Stanley Cavell and the Magic of Hollywood Films

This book is dedicated to the memory of Professor Stanley Cavell, its subject. His writings have enriched my life immeasurably, by introducing me to the philosophies of Emerson and Thoreau, and to the most creative account of the magic of the movies I have yet come across. I only hope it is as therapeutic to my readers as his work has been for me.

Stanley Cavell and the Magic of Hollywood Films

Dan Shaw

EDINBURGH
University Press

Edinburgh University Press is one of the leading university presses in
the UK. We publish academic books and journals in our selected subject
areas across the humanities and social sciences, combining cutting-edge
scholarship with high editorial and production values to produce academic
works of lasting importance. For more information visit our website:
edinburghuniversitypress.com

© Dan Shaw, 2019, 2021

Edinburgh University Press Ltd
The Tun—Holyrood Road
12 (2f) Jackson's Entry
Edinburgh EH8 8PJ

First published in hardback by Edinburgh University Press 2019

Typeset in 11/13 Monotype Ehrhardt by
Manila Typesetting Company

A CIP record for this book is available from the British Library

ISBN 978 1 4744 5570 1 (hardback)
ISBN 978 1 4744 5571 8 (paperback)
ISBN 978 1 4744 5572 5 (webready PDF)
ISBN 978 1 4744 5573 2 (epub)

The right of Dan Shaw to be identified as author of this work has been
asserted in accordance with the Copyright, Designs and Patents Act 1988
and the Copyright and Related Rights Regulations 2003 (SI No. 2498).

Contents

1 Introduction: Defining the Magic—Why Stanley Cavell? 1
2 Projecting Reality 7
3 Stanley Cavell: Emersonian Individualist 25
4 Cavell on Nietzsche: The Ascetic Ideal, Eternal Recurrence, and "Higher Self" 42
5 Comedies of Remarriage and the Transfiguration of the Commonplace 58
6 How the Unknown Woman Finds her Voice in *Contesting Tears* 76
7 Cavell and Wittgenstein on Skepticism: Redeeming the Law 93
8 Heidegger, Cavell, and Woody Allen: *Another Woman* 105
9 *Halls of Montezuma* and the Utility of War 118
10 Thoreau, Civil Disobedience, and *Selma* 129
11 Lockean Liberalism and *Mr. Smith Goes to Washington* 140
12 Cavell's Notion of Acknowledgment and *Boys Don't Cry* 151

References 160
Index 162

CHAPTER 1

Introduction: Defining the Magic—Why Stanley Cavell?

Figure 1.1

I have come to the work of Stanley Cavell late in life, as I have to the writings of Ralph Waldo Emerson and Henry David Thoreau. They have been a revelation to me, and an infusion of optimism that has helped me to overcome the anxiety of aging. They pursue a brand of philosophy that represents what is best and most progressive about the American spirit, making a singular and distinctive contribution to World Philosophy in the process. In the last decade or so, I have become an unabashed acolyte of their shared world view, and an advocate for Cavell's approach to talking about motion pictures.

Film theorists have sought to account for the magic of the movies in the Golden Age of Hollywood ever since the age ended with the breakup of the Studio system. I know of no one that has captured its essence as perfectly as Cavell. His twin theses, that film is the most realistic of artistic media, and that good movies share a common vision of the good (in Plato's sense of the term), go hand in hand. As realistic, the filmic medium is particularly effective in securing the suspension of disbelief on which the movies depend. The value system championed by classical Hollywood is a uniquely American one, the striving to better oneself through transformation that Cavell has identified as Emersonian perfectionism.

It is no accident that Hollywood films in the classical age embody these values; they are at the heart of the American Dream. Striving for social mobility (sustained by the myth that anyone, no matter how humble their background, can become President of the United States), and for our children to enjoy a better standard of living than we do, constitute that dream. The desire to better ourselves, and the faith that we can do so, have driven the nation since its founding. Striving to become who we are is the major task of the radical individualism and self-reliance so often lauded by American philosophers Emerson and Thoreau.

So I was inspired to write this book, to discuss Cavell's philosophy (and in particular, his philosophy of film) and its acknowledged intellectual precursors, and to propose original readings of films from a Cavellian perspective. My goals are to convince more film-philosophers to adopt Cavell's paradigm (as the best among several competitors in the field), and to popularize his point of view for the general public. My viewing experience in watching films has been immeasurably enriched by seeing them through Cavell's lens.

The structure of the book is dictated by these goals. It begins with a chapter on Cavell's general account of film as a uniquely realistic artistic medium, offered in *The World Viewed* (1971) and elsewhere, and his stunning insight that the content of a striking number of good Hollywood films share a vision of moral goodness. To illustrate the former thesis, I offer an analysis of *The Hurt Locker* (2009), which uses the realistic potentials of filmic representation to persuasively convey its thesis that war is a drug to which it is disturbingly easy to become addicted.

Two chapters on the philosophers who most influenced Cavell's world view follow. More than anything else, Cavell champions what he calls Emersonian perfectionism, striving for the "unattained but attainable self" that we all have the potential of becoming. As I do throughout, I allow Cavell to speak in his own words, quoting extensively from his published works. It may strike the reader as odd that in this, and in all the other chapters of the book, there are no quotes from secondary sources. Inspired by Emerson's warning that if all you do is quote from others there is nothing to learn from you, I have taken the unorthodox step (in film scholarship) of unpacking quotes from primary sources on my own, with no help from my philosophical colleagues. In so doing, I seek to allow those sources to speak with their own voices, and to develop my own voice in the process.

Cavell contends that striving for Emersonian perfectionism is what drives the female protagonists in both the remarriage comedies and the melodramas that he dedicated separate volumes to analyzing. I will demonstrate its relevance both to contemporary Hollywood films and to genres apart from the two he singles out by discussing how Katherine Graham in *The Post* (2017) takes the reins of her own life and determines the fate of the nation in the process, in one of the most stirring of Steven Spielberg's cinematic creations.

Friedrich Nietzsche is arguably the second most influential of Cavell's intellectual precursors. Like Cavell, Nietzsche acknowledged his profound debt to the writings of Emerson, and Cavell had a lot to say about Nietzsche as well. Nietzsche's imperative to become who we are, and his search for what he called a "higher self," resonated naturally with Cavell's Emersonian project. Nietzsche's famed (and notorious) concept of the Übermensch (literally "Overman," not "Superman") provides a useful template for what such a "higher self" might look like. I will illustrate their shared concept by applying a list of the purported traits of the Overman to an unforgettable cinematic character, Ada Stewart from *The Piano* (1993). A Victorian stranger in the strange land of mid nineteenth-century New Zealand, Ada arrives in complete control of herself, and soon exerts a similar degree of control over everyone around her. Her resolute will is depicted as indomitable, to an extent that even Nietzsche, despite his misogyny, might have respected.

My summary of Cavell's classic treatise on remarriage comedies, *Pursuits of Happiness*, will follow, the book that first hooked me on his approach to philosophizing about film. It focuses on his contention that such rom-coms are best suited to assuage our doubts about the validity of marriage, because they depict people who have questioned that validity, broken up, and choose to come back together again. It is also here that Cavell utilizes most persuasively his notion of acknowledgment, first introduced in his interpretations of *King Lear*. In his account, reconciliation of the romantic couple requires them to acknowledge the independent identity of the other, coming to know and respect each other through extensive conversations. I will have a good deal more to say about that notion in the Chapter 12. The chapter will show how relevant this theory remains to contemporary Hollywood films by applying it to *Eternal Sunshine of the Spotless Mind* (2004), one of the most beloved romantic comedies of the twenty-first century.

Analyzing Cavell's theory of the Hollywood Melodrama of the Unknown Woman in *Contesting Tears* is my next task. More than a decade after *Pursuits of Happiness*, Cavell returned to classical Hollywood to propose yet another genre theory that focuses on female protagonists searching for self-realization. What both the comedies and the melodramas have in common is the striving for Emersonian perfectionism. What distinguishes them is that their central women find themselves either within the confines of marriage or outside of it. I will try to further our understanding of Cavell's theory by questioning why he did not include *The Heiress* (1949) as one of his exemplars, although it fits his proposed profile in several ways.

This book is as much about Cavell's acknowledged intellectual precursors as it is about him, all of which are beloved by me as well. So, each of the next five chapters will feature what Cavell has to say about one such figure, discussions that are somewhat shorter than the analyses offered in Chapters 2 and 3. These will be followed by an original film reading that illustrates his philosophy, and Cavell's. I begin with Ludwig Wittgenstein, and Cavell's claim that at the heart of Wittgenstein's philosophy is a profound concern with skepticism. Cavell shares that concern, and contends that the remarriage comedies address our skepticism about the validity of marriage, while the melodramas assuage our doubts about whether women can find self-realization outside of marriage. I seek to broaden the relevance of Cavell's concerns by talking about films that address skepticism of a different kind, using *The Verdict* (1982) and the recent streaming miniseries *Goliath* (2016) to show how such "Redemptive Lawyer" films reassure us about both our justice system and the legal profession.

Martin Heidegger's influence on Cavell will be my next subject. Heidegger's notion of authenticity joins Emersonian perfectionism and Nietzsche's command to become who we are in the intellectual heritage of Cavell's quest to elevate self-realization as a moral consideration equal in significance to striving for the well-being of society as a whole (John Stuart Mill) and to doing our duty as we see fit (Immanuel Kant). The film reading here is a natural: the protagonist of Woody Allen's *Another Woman* (1988) is a female philosophy professor who has just published a book on Heidegger, and is striving for precisely the kind of authenticity about which Heidegger wrote. It also turns out to be a film that fits Cavell's blueprint of the melodrama of the unknown woman nearly perfectly.

Another form of skepticism that Hollywood films have often addressed is our doubts about the value of fighting a war, and of sacrificing one's life for one's country. So-called Pro-War films (many of which are made in times of war) seek to justify such sacrifices in various ways, primarily by showing that the war in question is just, and/or that the sacrifices involved are both necessary and valuable. Many of them reference John Stuart Mill's utilitarian moral philosophy, arguing that the costs involved in a war are outweighed by the benefits. One of the most explicit examples of this is to be found in *Halls of Montezuma* (1951) where Mill's hedonic calculus is frequently cited as the basis for the military's mode of operation. Cavell was quite fond of Mill as well, especially of his defense of the right to privacy and individuality and his disdain for conformity in *On Liberty*.

Henry David Thoreau was Cavell's other bellwether nineteenth-century American philosopher; he devoted an entire volume to his commentary on Thoreau's *Walden*. This chapter will discuss that classic, as well as the revolutionary treatise "On Civil Disobedience," in connection with Martin Luther King's successful attempt to put his principles into action. The recent Hollywood epic *Selma* (2014) celebrates such disobedience as leading directly to the Voting Rights Act of 1965.

Cavell dedicated an entire chapter of his book *Cities of Words* to John Locke because he incorporated Locke's theory that the basis of political association is the consent of the governed into his analysis of marriage as grounded in a similar form of consent. Skepticism about the machinations of Congress is, of course, nothing new, though it may be at its height in Donald Trump's America. Locke's theory of a workable democracy as involving three branches of government, two of which must be directly responsive to the consent of the governed, is stirringly championed in one of Frank Capra's most moving films, *Mr. Smith Goes to Washington* (1939). Jefferson Smith's use of the filibuster to block a graft-ridden deficiency bill shows how effective Congressional institutions can actually be. It is a film that bears re-watching at a time of unmatched cynicism about Congressional corruption.

The book concludes with a brief coda unpacking what I take to be one of Cavell's most fruitful contributions to the appreciation of Hollywood films, his notion of acknowledgment. I agree with him that mutual recognition of and from others, or the lack thereof, is crucial to the attainment of human happiness. This is particularly true for transgendered individuals, who seek to be recognized as who they really are by society as a whole. The lack of such acknowledgment has often been accompanied by both physical violence and mental abuse, from devout heterosexuals who seek to impose conformity on someone they believe to be utterly different from themselves. My last film reading will be of a poignant example of this process, as depicted in *Boys Don't Cry* (1999).

By the end of this book, I hope to have made the film-philosophy of Stanley Cavell (whose prose is not the most lucid)[1] more accessible to the general public. I trust that philosophers of film with an interest in Cavell will find this compendium of his philosophical influences useful. I also hope to have rendered his paradigm for how to philosophize about film more compelling, by extending it to eleven new exemplars. Finally, it feels good to gratefully acknowledge Cavell's extensive impact on my own approach to the philosophy of film.

NOTE

1. This is why you will find so many ellipses and bracketed inserts in the quotes: I have tried to clarify Cavell's intent whenever I can.

CHAPTER 2

Projecting Reality

Figure 2.1

> It must be the nature of American academic philosophy (or of its reputation), together with the nature of American movies (or of their notoriety), that makes someone who writes about both, in the same breath, subject to questions, not to say suspicions. (Cavell 1988: 3)

The attempt to understand Stanley Cavell's general theory of the nature of film must begin with his groundbreaking treatise, *The World Viewed*. Early on there, he contended that a canon of films must be established: "A standing discovery of the auteur theory was of the need for a canon of movies to which any remarks about 'the movie' should hold themselves answerable"

(Cavell 1971: 9). In his view, theorizing about the filmic medium helps us to form a canon, and vice versa. The need to specify a canon only becomes greater when you start talking about "the romantic comedy," or "the melodrama," and subgenres thereof, and Cavell addressed that need in the volumes that will be the next topics of my discussion.

The arts have long been seen as tracing an asymptote to the axis of reality, and part of the magic of film, according to Cavell, lies in its ability to most effectively project the illusion of reality. How do films "reproduce the world magically? Not by literally presenting us with a world, but by permitting us to view it unseen . . . we are displaced from our natural habitation within it, placed at a distance from it" (1971: 76). This identification of the viewer's position as one of both presence and absence is one of Cavell's deepest insights, grounded in the Kantian notion of aesthetic distance and Heidegger's claim that we tend to view the things and people around us as ready-to-hand equipment for our use. We see less than is there as a result, caring little for what those things and people are in themselves and focusing almost exclusively on how we can utilize them as tools to fulfill our needs.

Films allow us to see but remain unseen, free from the gaze of the others on the screen, and from the practical concerns associated with navigating their fictional worlds. This freedom and psychical distance permits us to indulge one of our deepest wishes: "What we wish to see in this way is the world in itself—that is to say, everything" (1971: 102–103). Freed from the tunnel vision that results from seeing the world as ready-to-hand, we are allowed to attend to other facets of being-in-the-world. Herein lies part of the magic of the movies: "What is cinema's way of satisfying the myth (of the world re-creating itself in its own image)? Automatically . . . satisfying it without my having to do anything, satisfying it by wishing. In a word, magically . . . movies arrive out of magic, from below the world" (1971: 76).

One of the major bifurcations in the history of theorizing about film was the clash between realists like Andre Bazín, who thought that the essence of cinema lies in its unique ability to capture reality continuously, and expressionists like Sergei Eisenstein, who privileged montage. This dichotomy raises:

> what many take to be the basic question on the subject, namely, whether it is the possibility of cutting from one view to another . . . or the possibility of continuous projection of an altering view (altered by depth of focus or by moving the camera) which is the essence of the cinematic. (1971: 73)

Both sides prescriptively argued that if this is what films do best, they ought then to do it more often.

Cavell sides with Andre Bazín in privileging the photographic essence of motion pictures, because this explains the unique impression of reality films can give us: "[What does it mean] [t]o say that a photograph is of the surfaces of objects . . . In order to reproduce the sights (objects) make, you have to reproduce them, make a mold, or take an impression. Is that what a photograph does? We might, as Bazín does on occasion, try thinking of a photograph as a visual mold or a visual impression" (1971: 69). It follows that:

> The material basis of the media of movies . . . is . . . a succession of automatic world projection. "Succession" includes the varying degrees of motion in moving pictures: the motion depicted, the current of successive frames in depicting the juxtapositions of cutting. "Automatic" emphasizes the mechanical fact of photography, in particular the absence of the human hand in forming these objects and the absence of its creatures in its screening . . . (1971: 72–73)

Film is such a credible medium because the photographic image and its object are identical.

While Cavell agreed with Bazín that the medium was uniquely realistic, he never tried to argue that film could provide the perfect imitation of nature that Bazín enthused about. Film can provide "views of reality," but not in its "virginal purity." It is always a representation of reality done from a certain perspective. But the realism of the medium was crucial to the attainment of the suspension of disbelief on which the Hollywood mythmakers depended.

Furthermore, for Cavell, film is a "moving image of skepticism." It has "a metaphysically hallucinatory character" by virtue of "causing us to see things that are absent. It makes things present to us to which we are not present" (Cavell 1996b: 69). Paradoxically, film can help save us from skepticism, and help reconcile us with the world in which we live. It does so by revealing to us the conditions of the possibility of subjectivity on which Cavell focuses. As we shall see, the most crucial condition is what Cavell calls "acknowledgment." Being a subject requires acknowledgment from another, and our skepticism about marital romance, to take one of his most prominent examples, is assuaged by watching two characters we root for achieve such mutual acknowledgment.

Cavell also refused to join Bazín in making the prescriptive claim that filmmakers should focus on doing more realistic films. He had a penchant for Hollywood fantasy, and for expressionistic film techniques: "movies, and writing about movies, have from their beginnings also recognized that film can depict the fantastic as readily as the natural" (1996b: 16). But Cavell thought inquiring about the nature of the filmic medium was worthwhile, especially in relation to agreeing on a canon of excellent films.

This is in stark contrast to cognitivist philosopher of film Noël Carroll, whose influential criticisms of what he called the specificity thesis (that the filmic medium is distinguished by a single specific thing it does better than any other medium, and ought to do more of) altered the conversation dramatically, and almost ended it. Carroll, in concert with David Bordwell, argued that speculation about the nature of the medium is fruitless, and that philosophers of film and film theorists should forgo theory and focus on the films themselves. Thankfully, the issue is far from being settled.

Cavell and Carroll have also come to stand for two competing paradigms of how to do philosophy of film, one broadly humanistic and the other grounded in the science of cognitive psychology. The stakes here are high:

> [The purpose of] defining "the medium of the art" is to help us to understand what has in fact been achieved and accepted within the various physical bases of an art, and [to determine] if the physical basis of movies, being irreducibly photographic, necessitates or makes possible the meaningful use of human reality and of nature as such. (1996b: 68)

A Hermeneutic circle exists between attempts to define the medium on the one hand and the founding of a canon on the other.

In a later, expanded edition of *The World Viewed*, Cavell identified a second crucial sense in which movies are magical: the movies tell mythical tales that inspire us in our everyday lives. This insight grounds his entire approach to genre theory. He sees films (and other works of dramatic art, such as Shakespeare's tragedies) as providing responses to the threat of skepticism. Films have the ability "to reveal reality and fantasy [not by reality as such, but] by projections of reality, projections in which . . . reality is freed to exhibit itself" (Cavell 1979a: 166).

Due to their perspectival nature, these "projections" inevitably highlight some features of reality and play down others, showing the elements variously in positive or negative lights:

> Often, it is the values that accomplished filmmakers self-consciously wish to champion that determine where those emphases are placed, and it is part of the task of the philosopher of film to identify those values. When engaged in interpreting the meaning of a particular movie, "Nothing—no variation or combination of angle, distance, duration, composition, and motions between—can be ruled out in advance as a sign of significance." (1979a: 204)

Their reason for championing the values they hold is not primarily moral. Rather, for the films that he addresses, "The question is not 'Why should I be moral?'—to which the answer may be that you are too cowardly for much of anything else. The question is whether the fate of goodness will be to lose its power to attract, whether all men and women will despair of happiness"

(1971: 59). One of the major values that combated that despair in the classical age of Hollywood was romance.

A decade before his treatise on the comedies of remarriage, Cavell pointed the way toward his eventual theory:

> So far we can grant that they might, the film reinstates the myth of modern marriage, which is the modern myth of romance . . . At some point, perhaps when the world went to war, society stopped believing in its ability to provide that continuity. It needed to know what modern romance asserted, that one couple can make it alone, unsponsored. (1971: 79)

In choosing to depict couples reunited in marriage after grave difficulties, the filmmakers were championing its value:

> What the country needed to know, in reduced circumstances was not merely that its [marriage's] legitimacy is being acknowledged, but that it is worth acknowledging. In particular, that it still allows those meant for one another to find one another, and that they can achieve happiness within the law. (1971: 79)

The two senses in which the movies are magical are complementary. Our tendency to take them as unmediated impressions of reality lends the myths their credence. We want to believe them, because we long to have our skepticism assuaged and our confidence in the values we hold dear restored. If Emerson is right, one of the major keys to human happiness is to feel that we are making progress toward our ideal self. Hollywood films in the Classic Age embody myths that tend to convince us that such progress is indeed possible. They are mythical precisely because they serve as such complete wish fulfillments: "The Capra and the Hitchcock films make nakedly clear the power of film to materialize and to satisfy . . . human wishes that escape the satisfaction of the world as it stands; as perhaps it will ever, or can ever, stand" (1988: 180).

Film is mythical despite the fact that it is the most democratic and pedestrian of the arts: it deals with, and speaks to, the common man. In speaking of this paradox, Cavell is reminded of:

> Thomas Mann's description, in his essay on Freud, of the "point at which the psychological interest passes over into the mythical," and of his assertion that "the typical is actually the mythical." . . . That gaze of knowledge is the province of camera and screen; it is the power that the director, in his pact with his audience—the mythical in the typical. (1979a: 178)

Cavell likens his appreciation of the typical to the ordinary language philosophy of Wittgenstein and Austin, his early study of which prepared him nicely to talk about the movies.

Psychoanalytically speaking, "film assaults human perception at a more primitive level . . . films' enforcement of passiveness, or say victimization, entertains a region not of invitation or fascination primarily to the masculine, nor even, yet perhaps closer, to the feminine, but primarily to the infantile" (1996b: 209). We are particularly susceptible to the cinematic arts, especially when they are screened in their appropriate venue, the womb-like darkness of a theater.

In "The Thought of Movies," his 1983 article in the *Yale Review*,[1] Cavell expands on his encomium to film by praising its unique power to express philosophical ideas:

> and I find in *The Awful Truth* that when the camera moves away from an imminent embrace between Cary Grant and Irene Dunne to discover a pair of human figurines marking the passage of time by skipping together into a clock that has the form of a house, that in that image something metaphysical is being said about what marriage is, that it is a new way of inhabiting time, and moreover that that is a way of summarizing the philosophy, among others, of Thoreau and of Nietzsche. (2005e: 7)

While this could be taken as a clear instance of a philosopher importing such meaning into a work that was far from intending to express it, this would be to miss Cavell's point, which is that films, and their ability to capture reality directly, often (though perhaps unintentionally) find objective correlatives for the deepest philosophical insights.

The movies bridged the divide between high art and popular culture with their universal appeal: "the medium of film is such that—from the time of its first masterpieces in the second decade of its technological establishment—it could take on the seriousness of the modern without splitting its audience between high or low, or between advanced and philistine" (Cavell 2005a: 14). It was Cavell's "persistent idea" that "the intervention of film in Western culture, especially perhaps in America, challenges our understanding of high art and low art, or of art and entertainment—which is not the same as denying the distinction" (2005a: 71).

Cavell contended that the finest moments in cinematic art, from a Fred Astaire dance routine to the ending of *The Awful Truth*, are of a comparable quality to the best works in any of the other artistic media. But their artistic quality is seldom appreciated: "It is my feeling that film has yet to attract a sharable critical discourse sufficient to its achievements" (2005a: 110). It was part of his mission to try to correct this insufficiency.

One of the most winning features of Cavell's writing is its sensitivity to how the various expressive tools of the medium convey their meaning. In discussing "The Camera's Implication," in connection with the point of view changing from a third-person to a first-person shot of Kirk Douglas as he walks through the trenches in *Paths of Glory*, Cavell insightfully describes its effect: "When the camera then moves to a place behind his eyes, we do not gain but forgo an objective view of what he sees; we are given a vision constricted by a numb and helpless rage" (2005a: 129).

In the next chapter of the original edition of *The World Viewed*, entitled "Assertions in Technique," he commented at length on several other examples. The use of slow motion (as Leni Riefenstahl discovered in *Olympia*) conveys an impression of lyricism. Ending television episodes, or feature films, with freeze frames, rather than the conventional outside pull-away shot, makes its point "by stopping the departing subjects in their tracks—partly returning the figures and their world to their privacy, but unable really to let them go . . ." (1971: 135). Attending to technique is more than "a matter of 'attending to details,' because the moral of art, as of a life, is that you do not know in advance what may arise as a significant detail" (1971: 145).

Cavell commonsensically observes that "since I find in movies food for thought, I go for help in thinking about what I understand them to be thinking about where I go for help in thinking about anything, to the thinkers I know best and trust most," like Emerson, Thoreau and Nietzsche (2005e: 9). Filmmakers and philosophers address the same complex realities of human existence, exploring them with images and arguments. There should be little wonder that they sometimes have remarkably similar things to say about them.

Cavell is sensitive to certain assumptions made by his critics, especially:

> The harmful way of charging my book with pretension takes it for granted that philosophy and Hollywood movies occupy separate cultural intentions, with nothing to say across their border, indeed with not so much as a border between them. The immediate harm in this view lies in its closing off an exploration of what those Americans to whom it matters may be said to have instead of a common inheritance of high culture . . . (2005e: 8)

The claim that philosophy and film "occupy separate cultural intentions" is based on an elitist notion of what it is to philosophize. Cavell, in contrast, urges a refreshingly egalitarian notion of what philosophers do:

> . . . what makes philosophy philosophy? I understand it as a willingness to think not about something other than what ordinary human beings think about, but rather to learn to think undistractedly about things that

> ordinary human beings cannot help thinking about, or anyway cannot help having occur to them, sometimes in fantasy, sometimes as a flash across a landscape; such things, for example, as whether we can know the world as it is in itself, or whether others really know the nature of one's own experiences, or whether good and bad are relative, or whether we might not now be dreaming that we are awake . . . Such thoughts are instances of that characteristic human willingness to allow questions for itself which it cannot answer with satisfaction. (2005e: 9)

Like all of us, filmmakers have pondered many of these unanswerable questions, and often address them, either consciously or unconsciously, in their creations.

Cavell is engaged in a therapeutic project in discussing both the philosophers and the films he chooses to write about. He argues that "contemporary philosophy is to understand its continuity with the ancient wish of philosophy to lead the soul, imprisoned and distorted by confusion and darkness, into the freedom of the day" (1988: 7). These films help illuminate that darkness:

> The implied claim is that film, the latest of the great arts, shows philosophy to be the often invisible accompaniment of the ordinary lives that film is so apt to capture (even, perhaps particularly, when the lives depicted are historical or elevated or comic or hunted or haunted). (Cavell 2004: 8)

We are more inclined to think philosophically in our everyday existence than we seem to be, particularly in the modern age. This is an important feature of these films, because "America [unless I specify otherwise, I use this term as shorthand for the United States], in refusing Emerson's bid for philosophy, has not to my mind sufficiently joined philosophically in measuring the value of our lives" (ibid.).

What is the proper attitude with which to address such issues? As he puts it:

> dogmatists will claim to have arrived at answers; philosophers after my heart will rather wish to convey the thought that while there may be no satisfying answers to such questions in certain forms, there are, so to speak, directions to answers, ways to think, that are worth the time of your life to discover. (2004: 9)

Filmmakers can point the way as well.

In "The Good of Movies," a speech delivered at the Center for Human Values at Princeton University in 2000, Cavell takes on the most crucial issue, from a philosophical perspective: what is the value of films? Should we simply appreciate their brand of relatively mindless entertainment, or can they do something more? Some might suggest that films can be useful didactic vehicles for educating the public about moral and political issues. But Cavell dismisses issue films as of less philosophical value, "because such films, whatever their considerable merits, tend to obey the law of a certain form of popular engagement that requires the stripping down of moral complexity into struggles between clear good and blatant evil" (1988: 334).

As he tells us, "my attention has over the years rather been attracted to cases that show film, good films, to have an affinity with a particular conception of the good" (ibid.). The "particular conception of the good" he had in mind was, of course, Perfectionism, which he claimed was embodied by many (most?) of the best films of the classical era: "the primary body of Hollywood films to be adduced here may be understood as inspired by Emersonian transcendentalism" (2004: 9).

One of his clearest examples of this philosophy being enacted in film is *Now, Voyager*:

> determine what her [Charlotte Vale's] view of her behavior betokens about her desires, which, according to my reading, has to do with her having outgrown the man, with aspirations that go quite beyond his sense [that she is nobly self-sacrificing] ... This is where the particular conception of the good for which an indefinitely large class of good films has an affinity comes in. It is the conception in what I have called Emersonian perfectionism ... (1988: 335–336)

Cavell's accounts of the particular comedies of remarriage and the melodramas of unknown women convincingly argue that these subgenres should be seen as such:

> I claim for these films that they are masterpieces of the art of film, primary instances of America's artistic contribution to world cinema, and that their power is bound up in their exploration of a strain of moral urgency for which film's inherent powers of transfiguration and shock and emotionality and intimacy have a particular affinity. (2004: 9)

This "moral urgency" has nothing to do with the Mill's hedonic calculus, or Kant's concern for doing one's duty for its own sake: "But when I thought about these eminent theories in connection with the lives depicted in the grand movies I had been immersed in, the theories and the depicted lives passed one another by, appeared irrelevant to each other" (2004: 11).

Part of Cavell's mission (and he was definitely "on a mission") was to enshrine the concern for becoming who we are as on an equal plane, morally speaking, to these other two most influential criteria in the history of moral thought. The issue with which the characters in these films grapple:

> [is] formulated less well by questions concerning what they ought to do, what it would be best or right for them to do, than by the question of how they shall live their lives, what kind of persons they aspire to be. This aspect or moment of morality—in which a crisis forces an examination of one's life that calls for a transformation or reorienting of it—is the province of what I emphasize as moral perfectionism. (Ibid.)

In representing the quest of Emersonian perfectionism so aptly, these films do a lot of good. They urge us to become who we are, and find our own unique voice. They assuage our doubts about the meaningfulness of our lives. They encourage us to take up the call to perfectionism, which "may be said to concentrate itself on the demand to make ourselves, and to become, intelligible to one another" (2004: 339). The progress that striving for perfection seeks is unique: "The Emersonian progress is not from coarseness to sophistication, or from commonness to prominence, but from loss to recovery, or, as Thoreau roughly says, from despair to interest, or as Kierkegaard and Heidegger and Wittgenstein and Lacan more or less put the matter, from chatter to speech" (2004: 340).

Films have the ability to remind us that "the power of questioning our lives, in, say, our judgment of what we call their necessities, and their rights and goods, is within the scope of every human being" (2004: 8). The protagonists in Cavell's favorite genres have often lost their sense of self, which they are seeking to recover. In other cases, they never had a clear sense of self to begin with. Discovering what Heidegger called an authentic form of speech rescues them from the depths of despair. This, in turn, calls for them to stop living in the they-self, becoming relatively indifferent to what others might think, and giving voice to their own deepest concerns.

Films can be surprisingly profound . . . one should never "underestimate the power of the medium of film to present events as credible whose comprehensibility requires and sustains meditation that goes beyond anything the film may know about itself" (2004: 116–117). That profundity has a primal power. In arguing against the feminist thesis about the hegemony of the male gaze in film, Cavell ventured to claim that:

> film assaults the human sensorium at a more primitive level than the (anyway the nontotalitarian) enforcement of an ideology can maintain. Film's enforcement of passiveness, or say victimization, together with its animation of the world, entertains a region not of invitation or fascination primarily to the masculine nor even, yet perhaps closer, to the feminine,

but primarily to the infantile, before the establishment of human gender. (2004: 259)

Film's appeal to the infantile level of human response has a great deal to do with its rhetorical force.

Each of the two genres that Cavell discusses at length addresses a particular form of skepticism. The comedies of remarriage reassure us about the validity and soundness of marriage; the melodramas reassure us that women can indeed fashion a productive life outside of marriage. In both types:

> the issues raised in these films concern the difficulty of overcoming a certain moral cynicism, a giving up on the aspiration to a life more coherent and admirable than seems affordable after the obligations and compromises of adulthood begin to obscure the promise and dreams of youth and the rift between public demands and private desires comes to seem unbridgeable. (2004: 13)

It is this ability to assuage our doubts that makes the movies so magical, and it is in their ability to secure the suspension of disbelief that they can do so.

This tendency of good Hollywood films to explore similar themes is not limited to the classical era. Cavell offers several contemporary examples of Emersonian perfectionism in action:

> It relates to such films in recent years of child (or adolescent) genius as *Little Man Tate* (1991), *Searching for Bobby Fischer* (1993) and *Good Will Hunting* (1997) . . . I understand their interest to lie in presenting genius as a metaphor for singularity, for what I earlier called the sage in each of us, that without which one cannot become the one one is; it is the single negation of elitism, namely, in being universally distributed, if for the most part buried in distraction and conformity. (1988: 343–344)

The best exemplar of what he is discussing is *Good Will Hunting*, where the (successful) goal of the analyst is to get the analysand to discuss his (highly traumatic) past, and to give voice to what he really wants out of life (in his case, to be reunited with his lady love by following her out to California).

Cavell concludes his case for this Emersonian thesis with more examples: "There seems to me a remarkable number of new films . . . that concern a quest for transcendence, a step into an opposite or transformed mood" (2005b: 344). He continues: "three of the five nominees this year [1999] for the Oscar for Best Picture can be seen as dealing with worlds counter to what Emerson calls the world of conformity, namely *American Beauty* . . . *The Sixth Sense* . . . and

The Cider House Rules . . ." (2005b: 345). He might have added *Boys Don't Cry* to his list, a 1999 production that I will discuss in Chapter 12.

This commonality of explored themes is wedded to the poetry of the movies: "I think of it as the poetry of film itself, what it is that happens to figures and objects and places as they are variously molded and displaced by a motion-picture camera and then projected and screened. Every art, every worthwhile human enterprise, has its poetry, ways of doing things that perfect the possibilities of the enterprise itself, make it the one it is . . ." (2004: 14).

The poetry of film is particularly well suited to the exploration of ordinary life:

> Any of the arts will be drawn to this knowledge, this perception of the poetry of the ordinary, but film, I would like to say, democratizes the knowledge, hence at once blesses and curses us with it. It says that the perception of poetry is as open to all, regardless as it were of birth or talent, as the ability is to hold a camera on a subject, so that a failure so to perceive, to persist in missing the subject, which may amount to missing the evanescence of the subject, is ascribable only to ourselves, to failures of our character . . . (Ibid.)

We appreciate the poetry of the everyday better when we experience it through the unique presence/absence of film.

Cavell would never presume to dictate what filmmakers ought to do on the basis of his ontology of film. Rather, he is exploring:

> the conditions of the possibility of films, something that in my first book about film, *The World Viewed*, I call film's material conditions. There I claim that significant films are ones that most creatively explore the implications, one could say the identity, of these conditions. To say that *Gaslight* and *La Captive* both explore the condition of the camera's invasiveness or power of surveillance or vampirism is meant to imply that no way is dictated in which film's conditions are explored by films, and that the discovery of more and less fruitful and original and beautiful ways of exploration, it is the obligation of criticism to respond to and to articulate. If such criticism were to be thought of, with pleasure, as philosophical, this would be a satisfaction to me. (2004: 99–100)

Hopefully, I will now engage in such criticism, by illustrating Cavell's claim that realism can be a good making characteristic in film with my reading of Kathryn Bigelow's *The Hurt Locker*.

Let me be clear about the sense in which I will argue that *The Hurt Locker* is virtuously realistic. Cinematic realism, in the first instance, refers to the verisimilitude of a film, especially to the believability of its characters and events. This realism is most evident in the classical Hollywood cinema that Cavell discusses so extensively. Ironically, ideological film theorists have argued that the techniques dominant in the classical age of Hollywood, including so-called "invisible" editing, central framing, narrative continuity, closure and the like, amount to a particularly beguiling form of illusionism. Cavell sees it in a different way, for that illusionism is at the heart of the convincing myth making in which classical Hollywood was engaged.

But the second form of realism depends mainly on the mechanical reproduction of reality by the camera that Bazín championed, and often ends up challenging the rules of Hollywood movie making. This is precisely the kind of realism featured in Bigelow's docudrama about the Iraq War. Like many such films, *The Hurt Locker* has an anti-war message, stated explicitly in its opening scene: war is an addictive drug. Let me explain why the particular brand of realism Bigelow chose serves her so well here.

The Hurt Locker shatters the most cherished Hollywood convention early on: it introduces us to its apparent protagonist, bomb defuser Sergeant Matt Thompson (Guy Pearce), only to kill him off in the first five minutes. This is crucial to communicate convincingly the film's core argument, which is that addiction to war is lethal. When Staff Sergeant William James (Jeremy Renner) enters the scene, his predecessor's fate hangs over him throughout, although he survives all of his encounters with IEDs.

Early scenes create a "you are there" quality in various ways. We see what is going on from multiple perspectives, including a closed circuit camera on the robot, the video camera wielded by an Iraqi civilian, jerky hand-held 16 mm cameras, first-person point-of-view shots from Sergeant James, and fixed platform shots from various angles. Rapidly edited, sequences feel as disorienting as they must be in real life.

Sergeant James is, in the words of a superior officer, "hot shit." He has disarmed 873 bombs in his tour of duty, saving countless civilian and military lives. Despite, or perhaps because of, his record, James is reckless, and lax about following orders. After all, when a Colonel calls him a "wild man" as a term of praise, what is he to conclude? Sergeant James has two wingmen in his squad that stand guard over him while he is doing his job, and he is supposed to keep in constant contact with them at all times. But when he doesn't want to hear their entreaties to exit an insecure bomb scene, he simply throws his headset out the window.

He does have a more human side to him, as shown by his interactions with an Iraqi teenager who hawks bootleg DVDs in the street. But everything within the military tells him that what he does is of ultimate value. The army psychologist reassures squad member Eldridge (Brian Geraghty) that "this doesn't have to be a bad time in your life. Going to war is a once in a lifetime experience." But Eldridge is more concerned with how much longer he has before he is finished with his rotation.

The other member of his team, Sergeant Sanborn (Anthony Mackie) is so worried that James is going to get them killed that he contemplates blowing his colleague up and making it look like an accident. But Eldridge will have none of it. They run into a band of British contract mercenaries with a flat tire, and get into a long-distance firefight with an Iraqi sniper. Sanborn takes over the sniper rifle when the contractor team leader is shot, but runs out of ammo rather quickly. James is absolutely cool under fire, as he and Eldridge have to clean off the bloody ammunition clip the leader was carrying. He doesn't blink when a fly lands on his eyelid. Meanwhile, Sanborn kills three of the Iraqis . . . he turns out to be quite a sharpshooter. Then Eldridge spots one trying to flank them and blows him away as well. The team works well together here. They party and roughhouse and drink when they return to camp, beginning to bond with one another.

Sanborn goes through James' possessions, and finds a picture of his child. It seems that he got a woman pregnant and married her not long before leaving for Iraq. He may or may not be divorced from her, though she is still living in their house. His inability to say for sure is a red flag indicating something is seriously wrong. James asks the other two about their romantic relationships, and Sanborn says there is a girl back home, but she insists they have a child together and he protests that he is simply not ready for that. Sergeant James also keeps souvenirs of his favorite disarmings, in the form of detonators from the sites. James and Sanborn start to roughhouse again, but then it turns serious, and Sanborn draws a knife, ending the confrontation.

With sixteen days left in their rotation, the team has the staff psychologist ask to ride along into battle (Eldridge had called him out on his inexperience earlier). They search an abandoned Iraqi outpost for unexploded ordinance, uncovering "a gold mine" of elements with which to make bombs. They also find the dead body of a young Iraqi that has been booby trapped. James disarms that too, pulling a block of C4 explosive out of the cadaver's chest. Outside, the psychologist moves several Iraqis off the street, then inadvertently detonates an IED that kills him immediately. Eldridge breaks into tears, realizing that it was at his prompting that his doctor got killed.

Will calls home when they get back to camp, but doesn't say a word when his wife picks up. He once again confirms his humanity by risking his life to go into town in civilian clothes and look for the young DVD salesman (who called himself Beckham, because he liked to play soccer). He fails to find the young man, and almost gets shot by his own troops when he returns out of uniform. He immediately goes out on a night time bombsite assessment mission, trying to determine whether it was a suicide bomber that did all the damage.

The site is sheer chaos, as our perspective is constantly changing with jump cuts from all different angles, while being illuminated by headlights, flares, spotlights, flashlights and flames. Sanborn sees it as the work of a suicide bomber, whose body they will never find in the wreckage of the bus. But James thinks it was detonated remotely, and wants to search the scene to find out from where. Sanborn protests that that's not their job, but James pulls rank on him and leads them on a hunt for the bomber.

Sanborn was right. Eldridge gets shot exploring one of the alleyways, and is carried off by two Iraqis. They shoot his captors, and get him back to camp with a serious leg wound. Needless to say, they did not find the one who detonated the bomb. James is clearly troubled by the outcome, and gets into the shower in full battle gear when he returns, breaking down emotionally. He comes out the next morning in a clean uniform and again in complete possession of himself, and makes little reaction when his DVD-hawking young buddy unexpectedly appears with more disks to sell.

As Eldridge is helicoptered out, in extreme pain, he tells his team that his femur is shattered in nine places, and that he will never walk again. He blames Will directly: "Fuck you Will. Fuck you. When we have to go out looking for trouble for you to get your adrenaline fix . . . Fuck you!" Eldridge is replaced on the team, and, with two days to go on his deployment, James takes on a suicide mission. A civilian has been locked into a metal vest full of bombs, and pleads with the Americans to get him out of it alive. Zoom-ins, frantic editing, and POV shots underscore and heighten the tension. James is unable to free the man, and gets caught in the blowback after the explosion. Bloodied, but not broken, he survives, and looks up into the sky at a kite flying overhead.

On the way back, James and Sanborn have a frank exchange. After protesting that he doesn't want to die, Sanborn admits that he has changed his mind about something important:

Sanborn: I want a son, I want a little boy, Will. I mean, how do you do it, you know? Take the risk?
James: I don't know, I just . . . I guess I don't think about it.
Sanborn: But you realize every time you suit up, every time we go out it's life or death. You roll the dice and you deal with it. You recognize that, don't you?
James: Yeah Yeah, I do. But I don't know why. Yeah. I don't know, JT. You know why I am the way I am?
Sanborn: No I don't.

Like most addicts, James has no idea why he is addicted.

The scene then changes abruptly back to Stateside, where James has returned after his hitch. He has to deal with mundane tasks like going to the grocery store, and cleaning out gutters, for which he is ill suited. He stands before an aisle full of cereal choices with a look on his face that says what can it matter which one he grabs. All too soon he is telling his wife about a terrorist bomb that killed fifty-nine in an Iraqi city, and that the army still needs more bomb specialists. Playing with his son is not enough, and before long he is in a helicopter going back into battle. The film ends with a shot of him striding confidently toward his next target in his suit of armor, with a look of complete contentment on his face.

The war movie is a type of action film, the general purpose of the larger genre being to generate excitement. Films of this kind are often described as providing an adrenaline rush, which is pleasurable in itself if there is no real danger to you and yours. The bombs pose no actual threat to the lives of the audience, and we know that . . . this is what provides what Cavell calls the aesthetic distance of viewing a film. It is present for us, but we are not present in it.

This is also the great challenge for action films. We know that we are not going to die if the heroes of *Fast and Furious* crack up in their cars. We are not going to burn up in the skyscraper fire, or be killed by bank robbers. But filmmakers must be able to generate adrenaline in us nonetheless. Here is where the realism of such depictions comes in. I have never been in combat, so I can only imagine how much adrenaline is produced in the average soldier. But I suspect that the real thing is about the most adrenaline-inducing activity one can engage in.

I grew up watching war films with my dad, both documentaries and fiction films. He had a marvelous BS meter that would register falsehood whenever he saw it in such films, and he would consistently praise the most realistic sequences. As he had fought the Japanese in the jungles of New Guinea, he knew whereof he spoke. He would have loved the Allied landing sequence that opened *Saving Private Ryan*, had he lived to see it.

Again, let me specify what I mean by "realistic," and what I don't mean. *The Hurt Locker* was taken to task by both veterans and critics for not being historically accurate in several ways, the most frequent complaints concerning the violations of military procedure it portrays. James' squad would not have been sent alone into an abandoned Iraqi facility that hadn't first been totally secured by ground troops. The military would never have tolerated a loose cannon like James, especially if Eldridge had reported that his squad leader got him crippled by sending him up an alleyway in search of a bomber. But the average filmgoer is by now fully aware of how historically inaccurate most films can be, and those are two of the strongest adrenaline-producing sequences in the film.

On the other hand, Oscar-nominated screenwriter Mark Boal based it on a story he wrote about the actual man who had disarmed the most bombs in Iraq. Furthermore, *The Hurt Locker* contains some of the most riveting battle scenes in the history of cinema, which capture what it must be like to put yourself so precariously in harm's way. It brought the second war in Iraq alive for the first time to most Americans, who didn't see much footage of our soldiers being killed by IEDs (censorship of war coverage was complete). The various cameras through which we view the film all carry with them the air of credulity gained by being direct recordings of (staged) reality.

For example, as in Vietnam, our soldiers in Iraq could not tell the difference between a civilian and a combatant, as anyone could trigger a bomb remotely with a cell phone or other detonator. This feeling that the threat could come from anywhere is skillfully conveyed by Bigelow, as she cuts from POV shots of the soldiers looking up at the civilians and them looking down on the Americans. As James tries to defuse the car bomb, his wingmen watch the civilians like hawks, trying to detect the one that would trigger the device before the bomb killed their compatriot.

The Hurt Locker's ability to successfully generate an adrenaline rush is crucial to attaining its essential purpose, which is to warn about the addictive quality of war. If it could not get us to feel the drug, we could never understand why anyone would become hooked on it. But Kathryn Bigelow is one of the best action directors in contemporary cinema, as she had already demonstrated in *Blue Steel*, *Point Break* and *K19 the Widowmaker*. It is ironic that the first woman to win an Academy Award for Best Director did so with a film about Alpha Male machismo in its purest form.

If the film is to achieve its goal, it must make us feel that James' decision to return to duty was a tragic one, which will inevitably cost him his life, or at the very least his humanity. He is incapable of transformation, and doesn't give family life a chance before reenlisting. By the time of the film's US release in July of 2009, it had become evident that the war in Iraq was a debacle, fought on false pretenses and destined to destabilize Iraq rather than restore order and democratic government. Audiences were more likely to see his sacrifices as pointless in light of this. This was not known in 2004, when the film is set, and when James' gung-ho attitude was easier to understand. He thought he was doing some good.

But the film makes it clear that this is not why he returned. Eldridge had him pegged: he was willing to do anything to keep those rushes coming, even if it meant abandoning his family, or breaking regulations and endangering his squad. James' remorse after getting Eldridge shot was real, but it did not stop him from returning to his deadly preoccupation. There is nothing to lead us to believe that he will be any less reckless in this tour of duty. His inability to change his life, as the opposite of Emersonian perfectionism, is a testament to the degree of his addiction.

So, there are many styles of cinema, and many purposes to which it can be put. Here is where Bazín was wrong and Cavell got it right. The specificity thesis in its prescriptive form assumes that all films are trying to achieve the same end; for Bazín, it was achieving the perfect representation of reality (as Hamlet put it, "to hold, as it were, the mirror up to nature"). Bazín thought realistic techniques as he understood them (like deep focus and long takes) were best at doing so, and concluded that more films should use such techniques. Cavell, on the other hand, had as much respect for fantastic films as he did for realistic ones, for either they were pursuing different purposes or there was more than one way to achieve the same purpose.

My contention is a simple one: however you define the term, realism is a virtue in cinema if it helps the filmmaker achieve his or her ends, and a vice if it inhibits that attainment. For Aristotle, moderation is a virtue because it is crucial to the attainment of happiness. In *The Hurt Locker*, realism is a virtue because it helps generate the adrenaline that the film hopes to warn us against. You can't fear what you don't feel.

To summarize the main points of the chapter, Cavell agrees with Bazín that film is one of the most realistic artistic media, but he does not go so far as to prescribe that the cinema should stick to realism. Rather, he argues that films can be of great value in urging audiences to reject a life of conformity, and to become who they are by giving voice to what really matters to them, and living accordingly. Cinematic realism, in the sense that classical Hollywood purveyed it, made films more convincing to their audiences, hence securing the suspension of disbelief that was crucial to doing so.

The movies can ally our doubts about what makes life worth living, and help us appreciate the poetry and preciousness of the everyday. This is truly the progress toward perfection that the human race longs for, and desperately needs. Otherwise, we will tend to despair and conform, "[a]nd Emerson and Thoreau are the writers I know best who most incessantly express this sense of life as missed possibility, of its passing as in a dream, hence the sense of our leading lives of what they call quiet desperation" (1988: 15). The films Cavell recommends reward our attention by inspiring us to turn away from skepticism and to believe in the power of individual transformation.

NOTE

1. This volume refers to the reprint in *Cavell on* Film (2005) edited by William Rothman.

CHAPTER 3

Stanley Cavell: Emersonian Individualist

Figure 3.1

> Eventually I would be able to note that happiness and happenstance spring from the same root, that the pursuit of happiness—whether this is an occasion for a step into selfhood or into nationhood—requires the bravery to recognize and seize the occasion, or as Emerson had put it, "the courage to be what you are." (Cavell 1988: 6)

What does it mean to say that Stanley Cavell is Emersonian? More than any other figure in the history of philosophy, Ralph Waldo Emerson served as Cavell's muse, inspiring his best and most poetic writing about film, philosophy and human nature. Cavell found the wellspring of his philosophy of film in Emerson's ideal of moral perfectionism. But, just as significantly, he found a thinker as obsessed with everyday life as he was, whose writings embody the perfect mix of seriousness and whimsy.

It is with the whimsical aspect of Emerson's world view that I wish to begin. In "The Thought of Movies," Cavell quoted approvingly from Emerson: "I shun father and mother and wife and brother when my genius calls me. I would write on the lintels of the door-post, Whim. I hope it is somewhat better than whim at last, but we cannot spend the day in explanation" (2005e: 18–19). Elsewhere, Cavell noted that Emerson was well aware that he was taking a risky approach to the world: "If we could know in advance of departure after whim that it will truly prove to have been our genius that has called us, then the gate to salvation would not be strait; there would be little need for faith, and little to write about" (Cavell 1992: 141–142). But he believed we should live dangerously, especially as philosophers:

> Emerson's passage . . . acknowledges his writing to be posing exactly the question of its own seriousness. In the parable I just cited, he both declares his writing to be a matter of life and death, the path of his faith and redemption, and also declares that everything he writes is Whim. I understand this to mean that it is his mission to create the language in which to explain himself. (1992: 19)

This theme in Emerson is pivotal for Cavell: to become who we are requires us to risk finding our own unique voice, justifying ourselves to the world by coming up with our own good reasons for why we are this way rather than that. This is the central task of the women in both the remarriage comedies and the melodramas as he reads them: to find their voices and declare their reasons. Emerson found his own unique voice, and articulated a philosophy that has helped shape a nation.

Emerson's way of going about this was ebullient, expressing an attitude that Cavell linked to the work of Fred Astaire:

> [Astaire's art] would then be a concrete translation of what such a thinker as Nietzsche meant by dancing (as when Zarathustra speaks, urging: "Raise up your hearts, my brothers, high, higher! And don't forget your legs! Raise up your legs, too, good dancers . . .!")—something I guess he would have learned, among other things, from Emerson.

Cavell continued by alluding to Emerson on the potential impact of philosophy: "'All that we reckoned settled shakes and rattles; and literatures, cities, climates, religions, leave their foundations and dance before our eyes.' Can an

Astaire–Rogers dance, projected on a screen, be this good? How good would this good have to be?—This is serious business" (2005e: 23).

Conformists seek to counteract the tendency to boisterousness that often emerges in the process of becoming who you are; synonymous with being lively, animated, exuberant, spirited, and rambunctious, boisterousness signals an aversion to conformity:

> reliance upon oneself demands, and provides in return, ways to confront those who guard and impose conformity . . . The demand of conformity would accordingly demand that I justify my wayward life (not at this stage criminal, but, say, critical, discomfiting), and the provision of justification, as exemplified by the self-reliance of Emerson's writing, takes the form of making myself intelligible to those concerned. (Cavell 2004: 4)

It is a fascinating notion, one that Cavell puts at the center of his philosophy of film genres, and of life.

Conformity robs life of meaning:

> I mean this to capture the experience of Emerson's saying . . . that conformity makes "most men" [meaning most to whom he feels he is responding], "not false in a few particulars, authors of a few lies, but false in all particulars . . . So that every word they say chagrins us and we know not where to begin to set them right." (2004: 6)

Emerson declared himself to be the resolute enemy of such conformity, and the champion of what Martin Heidegger would later call authenticity. Cavell described the challenge Emerson faced in monumental terms: "America has not yet been discovered. Then his task as a writer is to discover the terms in which it can be discovered. Then what will constitute its discovery? I make the following fundamental assumption: What I characterized as making oneself intelligible is the interpretation moral perfectionism gives to the idea of moral reasoning" (ibid.). Cavell believed that Emerson lived up to that challenge.

But many people fail to do what is required: "We might think of it as accepting responsibility for being the one you are, hence, as perfectionists may put the matter, for becoming it—and demanding this fundamental gesture from others. Without this acceptance of radical responsibility, as for each jot and tittle of one's deeds and words, politics tends toward the exchanges of ghosts" (2004: 180).

Cities of Words: Pedagogical Letters on a Register of the Moral Life is a later work, where Cavell revisits both of his central film treatises in lectures from a class on moral perfectionism that he taught at Harvard. There, he takes a backward glance at the theories and exemplars that he had seemingly analyzed so thoroughly, while addressing a few additional figures, and films. The result is a more mature take on both types of Hollywood movies, and one of his clearest accounts of the philosophy of Ralph Waldo Emerson and its relation to film.

There, Cavell relates Emersonian perfectionism to the context of traditional moral theorizing:

> A favored way of approaching the field of moral theory is to contrast two major theories: one of them, called deontological, takes the notion of right as fundamental . . . emphasizing the assessment of human action by its responsiveness to obligation and the motive of duty; the other of them, called teleological . . . emphasizing the assessment of human action by its responsiveness to the call to maximize pleasure or happiness . . . (2004: 9)

Perfectionism does not fit neatly into either of these two categories, however, because Emerson's concerns were quite different from those of Kant and Mill.

Cavell clearly shows that becoming who they are is the central concern in the remarriage comedies:

> The issues the principal pair in these films confront each other with are formulated less well by questions concerning what they ought to do, what would be best or right for them to do, than by the question of how they should live their lives, what kind of persons they aspire to be. This aspect or moment of morality—in which a crisis forces an examination of one's life that calls for a transformation or reinventing of it—is the province of what I emphasize as moral perfectionism . . . [i.e.] that aspect of moral choice having to do with, as it is sometimes put, being true to oneself . . . (2004: 11)

It is not accidental that the philosophers Cavell refers to most often have put something very like perfectionism at the heart of their respective philosophies. For Socrates, Emerson, Thoreau, Nietzsche, Heidegger, and Wittgenstein, there was no priority more pressing than becoming who you are, and they all offered therapeutic recommendations on how best to do so. And it was not just these philosophers.

In *Conditions Handsome and Unhandsome: The Constitution of Emersonian Perfectionism*, Cavell cites over a hundred works of philosophy and literature that are relevant to a discussion of this significant philosophical movement. Most of them have largely been left out of the conversation by professional philosophers. For example, despite the fact that "Emerson is a thinker with the accuracy and consequentiality one expects of a major mind" (Cavell 1996a: 354), it has been hard to get him to be taken seriously within the profession.

Unlike the empiricists, who thought our impressions were directly caused by the things that give rise to them, "In Emerson, my impressions are my interpretations of the world, the way I experience the world, the basis of my judgments of its worth, how it matters to me, impresses me, or not. What I am caused to do and what I am free to do are then subject to my investigation" (1996a: 371–372). Emerson's thinking was far ahead of its time in this regard, and helped inspire Nietzsche's perspectivism.

Furthermore, "Emerson's prose is in service of . . . a moral outlook that has largely lived in the disfavor of academic moral philosophy, when, that is, that philosophy has taken notice of it at all" (1996a: 354–355). Utilitarianism provides a way to calculate the good an action is likely to produce; Kantianism allows us to determine the rightness of an action in terms of its dutiful intent; but "[p]erfectionism proposes confrontation and conversation as the means of determining whether we can live together [and] accept one another into the aspirations of our lives" (1996a: 24).

These concerns are the proper province of moral reasoning, according to Cavell, because:

> Moral reasoning is [designed] . . . to take me from confusion to (relative) clarity in seeking a world I can want. Moral perfectionism challenges ideas of moral motivation, showing . . . the possibility of my access to experience which gives [shape] to my desire for the attaining of a self that is mine to become, the power to act on behalf of an attainable world I can actually desire. (1996a: 33)

In situations of consequential choice, striving for perfection is a consideration that should arise whenever I decide what I ought to do.

Doing so obliges me to found (and find) my own unique self, which is made possible only by what Emerson calls "self-reliance". Emerson's most famous essay "is written in aversion, aversion to conformity. And since the work of the word 'conformity' in this context is to name a virtue . . . the implication is that his writing on self-reliance exhibits or enacts a contribution to a counter way of life" (1996a: 17). The transition from conformity to self-reliance is by no means an easy one: "A mark of this stage is a sense of obscurity, to yourself as well as to others, one expression of which is a sense of compromise, of being asked to settle too soon for the world as it is, a perplexity in relating yourself to what you find unacceptable in your world" (1996a: 5).

For it is not enough simply to be a nonconformist . . . the mere nay-sayer gets stuck at the stage of the rebellious teenager, and never attains Nietzsche's vision of the creative child who says yes to life anew. In the Introduction to *Contesting Tears: The Hollywood Melodrama of the Unknown Woman*, Cavell quotes Emerson's striking image of the attitude of the self-reliant individual, who embodies "[t]he nonchalance of boys who are sure of their dinner, and would disdain as much as a lord to do or say aught to conciliate one is the healthy attitude of human nature" (1996b: 34). The nemesis of such world makers is "us seniors": "what Emerson calls innocence rebuking the terrible thing that had happened to us seniors with our 'experience', from which we learn nothing new" (1996b: 35).

But this innocence does not imply an infinite malleability. Although the most famous quote from *Self-Reliance* (n.d.: 11) is "A foolish consistency is the hobgoblin of little minds," Cavell notes that "I think it is worth following further with Emerson's idea of the self—in its aspect as mind—as a *consistency*" (1996b: 138, original emphasis). The remark is made in a long paragraph about Heidegger, and it sounds as if such consistency would involve what Heidegger deemed the virtue of resoluteness in the pursuit of one's authentic goals. Cavell continues: "Then the alternative to one consistency (call it that of fools) is not an inconsistency but a different consistency" (1996b: 139). It is foolish to live consistently according to outworn traditions, and wise to consistently pursue your own authentically chosen purposes.

The women Cavell discusses in his two genre treatises develop more character as their films unfold, and "The idea of 'character' in Emerson always refers simultaneously to something about the worth and stamp of an individual's . . . difference from others, and to physical traces of writing (or of expression more generally)" (ibid.). Cavell's women proudly declare their difference from the herd of desperate humanity, for all to see and hear. When she returns from her liberating cruise, Charlotte in *Now, Voyager* refuses to abandon her newfound style and selfhood at her mother's behest. She sticks with it, for she has found herself.

If Cavell were to have his way, then striving for self-reliance would join utility and rational duty as one of the three primordial sources of moral value, and as the fundamental criteria for moral reasoning. The command "To thine own self be true" needs to take its proper place alongside Mill's principle of utility and Kant's Categorical Imperatives, as delineating the primary concerns of anyone who seeks to be a moral person. For Emerson, as for Kant, "the foundation of morality, of the expression of my freedom, can also be said to be based on a law I give to myself" (1996b: 139). But, unlike Kant, "In Emerson's words mankind is still pictured as living in two worlds, but the worlds now are not those of nature and of understanding . . . but those of society as it stands and as it may become—hidden in, and in a struggle with, the present" (1996b: 141).

In a brilliant allusion to Plato's concept of education as ascent to enlightenment in *Republic*, Cavell points out "Emerson's related counter image . . . of our finding ourselves someplace on a series of stairs, perceiving those stairs below us that we have ascended, and those above us that we have not reached" (1996b: 315). Later, Cavell returns to the image, having talked about the various figures he discusses in the book as constituting such stairs: "The stairs Emerson pictures . . . are such that each is one on which we have *found*, and, in some measure . . . attained, some further reach of an attainable self" (1996b: 316). This is the impact he hopes *Cities of Words* to have: "The idea, or dream, of this book is that each of us will be enabled to take these steps in conversation with the successive pairs of works we have committed ourselves to" (2004: 316).

Cavell is also concerned with the creation of community, which has to do with the sharing of a language. Cavell agrees with Emerson (and Heidegger) that language plays a critical role in permitting us to see the world, and ourselves, as meaningful. All three sought (as Heidegger put it) to "transform the people's speech so that now every essential word carries on the struggle and sets up the decision of what is holy or unholy, what great and what small, what brave and what cowardly, what noble and what low, what master and what slave" (quoted in Cavell 1989: 14–15).

So, the notion that Emerson only cares about the individual is hogwash: "The endlessly repeated idea that Emerson was only interested in finding the individual should give way to . . . the idea that this quest was his way of founding a nation, writing its constitution, constituting its citizens" (1989: 93). Emerson challenges the true man to transform the world in light of his unique vision: "This experience necessitates the ending of the essay 'Experience' which accepts the question 'Why not realize your world?'" The answer of the final sentence—"The true romance which the world exists to realize will be the transformation of genius to practical power"—indicates that Emerson thought of himself as being something of a visionary: "Emerson's work presents itself as the realization of [a] vision" (1989: 165) of an America that can still realize its magical potential.

Using language poetically, edifying philosophers are often engaged in a process of valuation, showing people, activities, and things in a positive or negative light. If their language catches on, it can shape the consciousness of a people, as Cavell's has among the community of his adherents. It is against the backdrop of Emersonian perfectionism, and the role of inventing a new way of speaking in striving for it, that Cavell's philosophy of film must be appreciated.

The two central themes of moral perfectionism appear throughout Cavell's later writings: "This thought, implying our need of invention and of transformation, expresses two dominating themes of perfectionism. The first theme is that the human self—confined by itself, aspiring toward itself—is always becoming, as on a journey, always partially in a further state. This journey is described as education or cultivation." (2004: 8). He continues:

> The second dominating theme is that the other to whom I can use the words I discover in which to express myself is the Friend—a figure

that may occur as the goal of the journey but also as its instigation and accompaniment. Any moral outlook—systematically assessing the value of human existence—will accord weight to the value of friendship. But only perfectionism, as I understand it, places so absolute a value on this relationship. The presence of friendship in the films we will consider (including the sometimes drastic lack of this relation in the melodramas) is of the most specific importance in establishing them as perfectionist narratives. (2004: 9)

In the romantic comedies (like *The Awful Truth*), the central couple discovers that they are indeed the best of friends. Part of what makes the women in the melodramas unknown is their lacking friends, and their emergence as known persons is often catalyzed by such a friendship developing (for example, Charlotte's relationship with Dr. Jaquith in *Now, Voyager*).

Moral perfectionism, as articulated by Emerson, also has a third crucial trait: the search for it is genuinely philosophical. As noted earlier, Cavell is extremely concerned about the less than enthusiastic reception Emerson has received in the philosophical and critical community, which sometimes seems to deny that what Emerson said deserves the title of philosophy:

it matters to me because I do not want a text to be denied the title of philosophy on the ground that it does not exactly take the form you might expect of philosophy. The denial of the title tends to excuse the tendency to refrain from putting much intellectual pressure on Emerson's words ... it matters to the idea of moral perfectionism, which is somehow bound up with an idea of a philosophical way or imagination of life. (2004: 3)

Part of the problem of getting Emerson taken seriously as a philosopher has been the dominance of analytic philosophy in the second half of the twentieth century, which stigmatized poetic philosophizing as meaningless gibberish. Cavell condemned the movement in *The New Yet Unapproachable America*, because it believed that:

America's contribution to, or leadership in, the growing international effort to establish philosophy within or adjacent to the bank of the sciences, natural and cognitive, is philosophy enough for a nation. But that such an ambition leaves out the participation of the writers of my culture that do me the most good (Emerson and Thoreau, to begin with) means that it is not enough. (Cavell 1989: 83)

The rest of the problem may be that Emerson is so darned optimistic, perhaps the most optimistic writer in the history of philosophy. Unfortunately, this sunny disposition has been mistaken for superficiality:

> The point is the achievement not of affirmation but of what Emerson calls "the sacred affirmative" ("The Preacher"), the thing Nietzsche calls "the sacred Yes" ("Three Metamorphoses" in Zarathustra), the heart for a new creation. This is not an effort to move beyond tragedy—this has taken care of itself; but to move beyond nihilism, or beyond the curse of the charge of human depravity and its consequent condemnation of us to despair; a charge which is itself, Emerson in effect declares, the only depravity ("New England Reformers"). (1992: 133)

In Cavell's eyes, Emerson should be seen as one of our most profound thinkers:

> In my own case, my discovery, or rediscovery for myself, of Emerson and of Thoreau seems to me a kind of hearkening to Emerson's call to American scholars. When I ask whether we may not see them as part of our inheritance as philosophers, I am suggesting that our foreignness as philosophers to these writers (and it is hard to imagine any writers more foreign to our currently established philosophical sensibility) may itself be a sign of an impoverished idea of philosophy, of a remoteness from philosophy's origins, from what is native to it. (1992: 148)

As with the originators of philosophy, like Socrates and Plato, Emerson's primary task is edification, in the sense in which the Merriam-Webster online dictionary defines it: "the instruction or improvement of a person morally or intellectually." He seeks to improve his readers morally by calling upon us to become who we are. He seeks to instruct us about the limitations of our intellect, while sharpening it by demanding that we stand and deliver on our convictions, in ways that only we can adequately express, and make intelligible to others.

Emerson was also a transcendentalist, and believed that edification involved teaching people to rise above the lower animalistic impulses of life (animal drives), and move from the rational to the spiritual realm. On his view, the human soul is an aspect of an overarching Oversoul or universal spirit, to which it and other souls return at death. Every individual is to be respected as a participant in that Oversoul. This Oversoul or Life Force or God can be found everywhere, in both nature and human nature.

But, as central as they are, Cavell never discusses these tenets of Emerson's world view at any length, except for noting the existence of a "transcendental mood" in Emerson's writings, which he describes as "the experience of an ecstatic possibility, as of another world adjacent to this one that this one speaks of in a homely symbol" (Cavell 1981: 109). Other than that, Cavell dismissed the supernatural trappings of transcendentalism outright. In *The Senses of Walden*, for example, he demurs: "I am not unaware that this may sound like one of those Transcendentalist sublimities which I confessed a while ago has seemed repellent to me, no doubt significantly because they may seem so easy for someone to voice who has Emerson's connections [with organized religion]" (1992: 158).

In an interview with the *Harvard Review of Philosophy* in 1999, Cavell addressed the religious overtones in Emerson:

> Well, the idea of Emersonian Perfectionism is certainly one for me that invokes philosophy, not simply in connection with life . . . but even more startling, philosophy itself as a way of life. Both these relations of philosophy to the way one lives are in Emerson, and, in that way, he picks up a very large, long, fascinating, honorable tradition of philosophical thinking. It is in itself no more religious than it is . . . I don't know that I'd say [that Emerson's body of work provides] quite a substitute for religion, but it becomes a part of philosophy's quarrel with religion, a quarrel or competition with religion in forming some basis for human existence. Emerson, after all, left the pulpit when he was in his thirties. (Cavell 1999: 22)

By contrast to the rather dour Unitarianism which he abandoned, another trait of Emerson's that Cavell recommends we emulate is his cheerfulness: "And yet Emerson clearly regards himself as exercising the duties of the American scholar, i.e. of Man Thinking, which he finds to be comprised in self-trust, soon to be renamed by him self-reliance. Along with guiding men, the office of the scholar is to cheer and to raise them" (2004: 159). Both sought to challenge their readers to live authentically, and to give them the confidence to do so. Guiding men requires a type of genius, as Emerson described in *Self-Reliance*: "To believe your own thought, to believe that what is true for you in your private heart, is true for all men—that is genius. Speak your latent conviction and it shall be the universal sense; for always the inmost becomes the outmost" (quoted in 1992: 138).

Rather than dwell on their transcendentalism, then, Cavell construes Emerson and Thoreau to be precursors of ordinary language philosophy:

> This sense of being able to speak philosophically and openly about anything and everything that happens to you is an ideal of thinking that first seemed to me possible in contemporary professional philosophy in the work of the later Wittgenstein and in that of J. L. Austin . . . their

redemption of what they call the ordinary from its rejection in much of philosophy has perhaps most importantly meant to me. (2004: 11)

Sharing their attitude inclined Cavell to talk about films philosophically early on, when discussion of "mere entertainment" was not thought to be intellectually respectable, especially in philosophical circles. What could be more everyday than talk about the movies?

Film, as an artistic medium, was made for philosophy: "it shifts or puts different light on whatever philosophy has said about appearance and reality, about actors and characters, about skepticism and dogmatism, about presence and absence" (1999: 25). In the Introduction to *Pursuits of Happiness*, Cavell discusses the affinity between Emerson and film: "Here I should like to add that without the mode of perception inspired by Emerson (and Thoreau) of the everyday, the near, the low, the familiar, one is bound to be blind to some of the best poetry of film" (1981: 15). This is crucial to his understanding of the nature of the remarriage comedies, for "It is to the point that the genre in question in this present book in the end will become characterizable as a comedy of dailiness" (ibid.).

To turn from everyday concerns to historic ones, Steven Spielberg is, to my mind, the most eloquent purveyor of Emersonian perfectionism in contemporary cinema. His most recent critical triumph, *The Post* (2017),[1] is a brilliant example of Emerson's philosophy in action. It tells the story of Katherine (Kay) Graham (Meryl Streep), the first woman to own a major metropolitan newspaper, and her momentous decision to publish the Pentagon Papers in the *Washington Post* after the US Government had blocked the *New York Times* from doing so. Her decision established her status as a publisher to be reckoned with, and her paper as a voice listened to around the world. I offer this interpretation of *The Post* to demonstrate Emerson's continued relevance to the appreciation of modern Hollywood.

The film opens in Vietnam, where Daniel Ellsburg (Matthew Rhys) was embedded with an American platoon that engaged in fierce firefights. He reports to his superior, Secretary of Defense Robert McNamara (Bruce Greenwood), that he believes things are getting worse over there. The Secretary agrees with him, then lies to the press and puts on a hopeful façade. This leads Ellsberg to steal and copy what would come to be called the Pentagon Papers, a sheaf of government documents proving that the US knowingly conducted a war that it could not win, while perpetrating a bevy of illegal acts (and international war crimes) in the process.

We then cut to publisher Graham, waking up with a start in the middle of the night. Having inherited a controlling interest in the paper when her predecessor husband killed himself, she is preparing to take the corporation public for the first time, selling shares whose price will determine the future of the paper. In a competitive market, the paper is cash poor, and she wants to hire more experienced reporters, arguing that quality and profitability go hand in hand. Her financial consultants are not as sure of this as she is.

She has lunch with managing editor Ben Bradlee (Tom Hanks), who has a mind of his own and won't agree to send a less controversial reporter to cover the wedding of President Nixon's daughter after he banned their present White House beat reporter from attending. Meanwhile, Ellsburg has contacted the *New York Times* and sends them the first sheaf of papers. Neil Sheehan pens a sensational initial report, and the *Times* is prepared to run it as a front page story.

Bradlee sniffs that something is in the wind, and sends one of his cub reporters to go to New York and find out what Sheehan is up to (an illegal activity). He meets with his staff, and comes up with a way to cover the wedding without sending a reporter. He proposes they contact the major newspapers that are covering it and ask them to share their notes. He suggests that they should make it a First Amendment thing, saying their competitors should be told that "[t]he only way to protect the right to publish is to publish."

Ms. Graham next confronts her skeptical Board of Directors, who want to lower the price of the shares in the initial offering, saying some of their prospective investors doubt whether the *Post* can ever become a substantially profitable enterprise. She hesitates to make her case that profit and quality go hand in hand, leaving it to her trusted colleague Fritz (Tracy Letts) to state the argument. This is a clear indication that she has not yet found her voice on the Board.

We learn why after the meeting, when the chairman explains to her that the investors are spooked about having a woman in such a position of power. He suggests that she share more control of the business with these investors, while it had up to now been a family paper, with a controlling interest owned first by her father, then by her husband, and now by her.

The cub reporter penetrates the *Times* by posing as a messenger, but learns little. Then Katherine's old friend Secretary McNamara gives her a heads up at a dinner party that the *Times* was going to run a bombshell article about him the next day. The first installment of the Pentagon Papers reveals that McNamara had believed the Vietnam War was unwinnable for six years, since 1965. It causes a national sensation, and leads Nixon to demand that further revelations be quashed. Bradlee is incensed that he has been scooped again.

He goes to Katherine, and tells her to ask McNamara to give her a copy of the 7,000-page Pentagon Papers. She refuses to do so, for reasons of personal loyalty, and when Bradlee tries to argue she has a greater obligation to both the paper and the public, she points out that Bradlee went easy on his close friend John F. Kennedy for the same reason. She refuses to let Bradlee push her around, for he is her employee.

Unexpectedly, an anonymous hippie chick brings in a big chunk of the controversial government report and hands it to one of the *Post*'s reporters. They're back in the game. Sheehan is way ahead of them, but then the Nixon White House secures an injunction banning the *Times* from publishing further excerpts from the papers, on grounds of National Security, and under penalty of incarceration. When Katherine first hears this, she assumes the game is over, but Bradlee proceeds with his plans to publish articles about them in the *Post* nonetheless.

The stock offering is made, at the lower price per share, and it is a success. Ellsburg is contacted by a reporter from the *Post*, and agrees to make all forty-seven volumes of the report available to them if they will publish despite the injunction. Bradlee interrupts Ms. Graham's birthday party to ask her if she will consider publishing the papers despite the injunction. The prospect panics her, because if the paper is held in contempt of court and its publisher and editor are incarcerated within a week of the sale, the language in the stock options grants investors the right to withdraw their money as they see fit.

Bradlee also thinks she hesitates at the prospect because of what the revelations would do to the stature and reputation of her friend McNamara. Recalling their earlier exchange, Bradlee tells her he was there to meet the Presidential plane that brought JFK's body back from Dallas. Despite his earlier connection to the Kennedy family, Jackie was adamant that none of what he observed that night was ever to be reported on or published. She did not trust him, and with just cause. As he put it, one can't be both friend and journalist. At crucial moments, you have to choose, and the duty of a journalist is to choose serving the public over one's private concerns. This was especially true since McNamara's study proved that four Presidents had lied for thirty years about that war. As Bradlee puts it: "We have to be the check on their power. If we don't hold them accountable then, my God, who will?" Graham does not immediately make up her mind.

Troubled by the choice she faces, she awakens from an impromptu nap face down at her desk and looks up at a convivial picture of McNamara and her at a social gathering. She decides to discuss it with him personally, and asks him straight out how he could have lied to the American people for so long. He spouts the party line about the domino theory and the plan to drive Ho Chi Minh to the bargaining table, and she remains unimpressed. She had sent her own son to fight in Vietnam, and now she has learned that it was all for the sake of America saving face in a war that it was destined to lose. She is blunt with him: "You were a fraud. That's what your study says." Then she gives him a heads up in return . . . she has the papers, and a big decision to make. Telling him she is asking for his opinion and not for his permission, he counsels her not to publish, both for his sake and to avoid being crushed by Nixon, who had wanted to ruin the paper for decades.

Her decision is further complicated by the opinion of the *Post*'s legal experts that the courts have the right to block publication on the basis of the Espionage Act. Fritz, her right-hand man, tells her they can't publish legally, while Bradlee argues that they can. Reporters are threatening to resign if they don't publish the papers, and Bradlee argues that the *Post*'s reputation will be ruined if it becomes known they had the report and didn't use it. He rehearses his earlier litany, that the only way to protect the right to publish is to publish. If both the *Times* and the *Post* cave in to pressure from the Nixon White House, freedom of the press will be dealt a lethal blow. Finally, Graham makes a decisive call: "Let's go! Let's publish!"

Legal concerns remain, including facing the charge of collusion because the source for the *Times* and the *Post* (Daniel Ellsberg) was the same. That would amount to contempt of court. The chairman of her Board of Directors urges Graham to stop publication before the first story runs, and Bradlee shares his anxiety with his wife that this could cost him his job and Katherine her paper. He knows that the paper could literally close forever if the government wins. But, as he said earlier, "if we live in a world where the government could tell us what we can and cannot print, then the Washington Post as we know it has already ceased to exist."

Ben's wife Tony (Sarah Paulson) reassures him that he can get another job, and that his reputation will only be enhanced by this decision, no matter what the outcome. As a woman, she appreciates the bravery Graham is showing:

> Kay is in a position she never thought she'd be in. A position I'm sure plenty of people don't think she should have. And when you're told time and time again that you're not good enough, that your opinion doesn't matter as much, when they don't just look past you, when to them, you're not even there, when that's been your reality for so long it's hard not to let yourself think it's true. So, to make this decision, to risk her fortune and the company that's been her entire life, well, I think that's brave.

In a sexist society, the default position of women is to be treated as less than, and as having a voice that doesn't matter. To make this decision to become who she potentially is requires her to forget what others have said and how they have treated her, and to refuse to conform to the gender stereotype of women as passive, silent and submissive to the wishes of men.

The scene changes to Katherine's daughter's bedroom. Graham had kept a series of suggestions her daughter had made for her first address to the Board of Directors, and insists that her daughter read them aloud. Number three recommends that Katherine say: "I never expected to be in this situation." She explains that her deepest desire was to hold on to the paper for the sake of her children, who would inherit it eventually if it remained a family-controlled enterprise.

Graham confirms a good deal more of Tony's speculations about what was really going on:

> No, but that's the way we all thought then. You know. I was never supposed to be in this job. When my father chose your dad to run the company, I thought it was the most natural thing in the world. I was so proud because, you know, Phil was so brilliant and he was so gifted and I thought that was the way it was supposed to be. Everybody thought that way then. And I was raising you kids and I was happy in my life the way it was. But then when it all fell apart, you know, when Phil died, it was just . . . I was forty-five years old I'd never had to hold a job in my life.
>
> But I just, I loved the paper, you know, I do. I do so love the paper.

As she concludes her talk with her daughter, having shared how scared she is that the paper might close, Ben arrives to inform Katherine that the same source collusion charge could lead to a contempt of court felony conviction and prison time. For the first time, he tells her he appreciates what she has at stake . . . the type is being set on the story, but she could still stop publication at the last moment.

Fritz and the chairman of her board both continue to urge her to back off, warning again that her stockholders will withdraw their financial support. But she finds her voice, and is heard loud and clear: "The prospectus also says that the newspaper will be dedicated to the welfare of the nation and to the, uh . . . principles of a free press . . . So, one could argue that the bankers were put on notice." When someone protests that these are extraordinary circumstances, Graham asks: "Are they? Are they? For a newspaper? One that covers the Nixon White House?" On that note, Fritz recognizes that it is her decision, and stops arguing with her.

She turns to Bradlee for reassurance that they will not cause the deaths of US soldiers by publishing. When the chairman interrupts her (as men in power have always done all her life), she cuts him off by reminding him she is talking to Ben. When he protests that she is forgetting her legacy, she retorts: "This company has been in my life for longer than most of the people working there have been alive so I don't need the lecture on legacy. And this is no longer my father's company. It's no longer my husband's company. It's my company. And anyone who thinks otherwise probably doesn't belong on my board." Case closed. Insisting that her decision stands, she goes to bed, and the edition goes to press. Fritz, though she has rejected his advice, has a nodding grin on his face, recognizing that his friend has come into her own.

The rest, as they say, is history. The government accuses the *Post* of violating the Espionage Act, and the case very quickly goes to the Supreme Court. But newspapers across the country have already followed the courageous publisher's lead and picked up the story. The *Post* had found its voice as a major national news source, and not just a little local paper. At the Supreme Court, a young government worker shows Katherine to her seat, and tells her of a brother who is fighting in Vietnam at the moment, and expresses hope that she will win her case. When it is over, she passes a number of young women who obviously also look up to her as a role model.

The verdict, 6–3 in favor of the right to publish, is read aloud in the newsroom, as is an excerpt from Justice Black's majority opinion: "The Founding Fathers gave the free press the protection it must have to fulfill its essential role in our democracy. The press was to serve the governed, not the governors." Katherine shares the triumph with Ben:

> Do you know what my husband said about the news? He called it the first rough draft of history. That's good isn't it? Oh, well, we don't always get it right, you know. We're not always perfect but I figure we just keep on it, you know? That's the job, isn't it?

He quietly, and admiringly, agrees.

The film ends with Nixon telling someone that from now on, no reporter from the *Post* will be allowed in the White House, and final shots of a policeman discovering the Watergate break in. The next chapter in this saga is, of course, told in *All the President's Men*. Who knows what would have happened had the *Post* failed to publish the Pentagon Papers. The Woodward and Bernstein exposé of Watergate might never have happened, and Nixon might never have been forced to resign in deserved disgrace.

In an era when President Donald Trump vilifies and scapegoats major news media as much as Nixon did, *The Post* is a timely reminder of the importance of the freedom of the press. But it tells a more perennial, and universal, tale of someone special becoming who they are, seizing the reins of power, and doing good. More specifically, it is the feminist tale of a woman overcoming the prejudices of a sexist society and taking command of both her own fate and the fate of a nation. *The Post* also illustrates Cavell's point that Hollywood films and philosophy are made for each other because the movies are such good embodiments of Emersonian perfectionism in action.

As quoted earlier, Cavell's primary answer to the question "What good is film?" is that "good films have an affinity with a particular conception of the good," namely, with Emersonian perfectionism (Cavell 2005b: 334). The myths that these films tell still sustain our faith in idealism in general, and in the value of marriage for some, and total independence for others. As a body of work, they constitute one of the richest and most uniquely American contributions to the history of culture.

NOTE

1. For script of *The Post*, see https://www.springfieldspringfield.co.uk/movie_script.php?movie=the-post (accessed February 27, 2019).

CHAPTER 4

Cavell on Nietzsche: The Ascetic Ideal, Eternal Recurrence, and "Higher Self"

Figure 4.1

> Let me attract attention to another untaken path here, on which one becomes extremely sensible of the causes of Nietzsche's love for Emerson's writing. I am thinking now of Nietzsche's *Ecce Homo*, a book about writing that bears the subtitle *How One Becomes What One Is*. Its preface opens with the declaration that the author finds it indispensable to say who he is because in his conversations with the educated he becomes convinced that he is not alive. The preface continues by . . . warning that to read him is to breathe a strong air. (Cavell 1996g: 307)

Although I was a Nietzsche scholar in my early career, it was Stanley Cavell who first called my attention to Walter Kaufmann's observation that Friedrich Nietzsche often carried a copy of Ralph Waldo Emerson's *Essays* on his person. I was aware of Nietzsche's references to Emerson (including sections by that name in both *The Gay Science* and *Twilight of the Idols*), but no one else, to my knowledge, makes as much of Nietzsche's debt to Emerson as does Cavell, characterizing it as equal to his own. He highlighted an example of that indebtedness that I had not recognized on my own: Nietzsche's concept of the *Übermensch* (which Kaufmann translated as "Overman" and not the more controversial "Superman") was clearly influenced by Emerson's essay on "The Over-Soul." This chapter will survey Cavell's pronouncements on Nietzsche, made mostly in connection with Emerson. My goal is to demonstrate that Nietzsche was almost as influential as Emerson in shaping Cavell's philosophical project.

Nietzsche was one of the philosophers Cavell referenced most frequently in his writings about film. He had good reason to do so. Along with Thoreau (and, to a lesser extent, Martin Heidegger), Emerson and Nietzsche anchor Cavell's overall philosophy, and his take on the meaning and value of the films he discusses. Indeed, he makes frequent tandem references to Emerson and Nietzsche. Central to both their projects was "the task of claiming your own existence, the thing Emerson and Nietzsche follow the Romantics (harking back to the Greeks, to Pindar) in describing as 'becoming who you are'" (2004: 191).

Let me try to distill the essence of Nietzsche's philosophy, as Cavell saw it, by unpacking the meaning of the following quotations, in order to understand why he took Nietzsche to be so relevant to his accounts of popular film. Cavell speaks most extensively about Nietzsche in a chapter in *Cities of Words* on "Schopenhauer as Educator" (one of Nietzsche's early "Untimely Meditations"). There, he notes several common themes in Nietzsche and Emerson: "these links are real in connection with such guiding concepts as culture (together with its debasement), and genius (together with its evasion), transfiguration and conversion and conformity" (Cavell 2004: 190). Cavell brings their common concern for the preservation of artistic culture to his discussions of the movies, the best of which can, in his estimation, stand shoulder to shoulder with the great literature and art of any age.

These philosophers also urge us to engage in a quest for originality, as crucial to fashioning our own unique self:

> The problem of imitation haunts philosophy's establishment in Plato, and in a further form it is in full flower in the work of Emerson and the work he inspired in Nietzsche . . . It arises in the question whether I have found the identity of my voice, whether I am saying what I think or

only quoting some saint or sage. And it arises in the question whether the
human world exists. (2004: 191)

Living at second hand, only quoting the thoughts of others, is a symptom of
the failure to create such a self. In that event, no one will learn anything from
you that they couldn't glean from the books you quote.

Cavell expands on the importance of this notion of self-creation, crucial to
his (and Emerson's and Nietzsche's) philosophical project of defending the
worth of human existence:

> Nietzsche actually uses the term "metaphysics" in "Schopenhauer as
> Educator," where he attractively uses the idea of man's "metaphysical dis-
> position" as his demand to answer the question "What is existence worth
> as such?" "Do you affirm this existence in the depths of your heart?"
> That is a question Emerson was equally determined to raise. (2004: 196)

This quest to become who we are is so crucial to human existence because, as
Nietzsche puts it, it is "the place of *Ursinn* [literally, the origin of meaning],
which may be taken as a primordial demand for sense, a demand as original and
clear as a baby's cry" (2004: 200). Individuals need to make sense of their lives
in order to give them meaning, and doing so requires expressing that sense in
their own unique terms.

Emerson and Nietzsche also shared the conviction that their time was out of
joint, and that it was up to them to try to put it right:

> But in Emerson and Nietzsche, the human beings we know, hence the
> human institutions we participate in, are, with certain exceptions, as such
> infected with unreality. And there are no instances of the human, in some
> realer or higher state, in some other realm. We are what, here and now, is
> what there is of the human, and we are, or it is, lacking; we are not what
> we are meant to be, not what the human expects of itself. (2004: 192)

But both were convinced that we could become that something more, though
we might well fail to do so.

Cavell believed that Nietzsche's writings are particularly relevant to answer-
ing one of our most urgent questions about cinema:

> Nietzsche's text is painfully pertinent to assessing what we might call the
> cultural standing of movies. Are they inherently part of low or popular
> culture, where this might mean that they are comprehensible only as
> some mode of entertainment? Or are they as various in quality and design
> as the things called books are, namely some of them belonging to low,

others to high, culture? Or is that distinction of service only outside the range of Hollywood films, which are as such low? Or is the distinction between high and low now out of service altogether, since the advent of what is called post-modernism? (2004: 208)

Cavell's treatises on Hollywood comedies and melodramas are both concerned to show that the films of which he speaks attain the level of high art, despite being the products of popular culture.

In *Pursuits of Happiness*, Cavell begins his analysis of the debased critical status of romantic comedies by attempting to explain why the search for happiness has acquired such a bad reputation. He references Nietzsche in order to do so: "Such comedies invite us to think again, what it is Nietzsche sees when he speaks of our coming to doubt our right to happiness, to the pursuits of happiness . . . [He sees] this repressed right as the construction of the ascetic ideal" (Cavell 1981: 131). According to Nietzsche, the hegemony of the Christian religion in Western culture led to a denigration of life on earth, and the pleasures that make it worth living were transformed into the Seven Deadly Sins.

Under the influence of the ascetic ideal, self-denial takes the place of self affirmation, and our uniqueness is endangered thereby. Cavell quotes Nietzsche in *Cities of Words* to underscore the depth of the crisis: "How does the philosopher [whom Nietzsche contrasts here with what he calls contented professors of philosophy] view the culture of our time? . . . He almost thinks that what he is seeing are the symptoms of a total extermination and uprooting of culture. The waters of religion are ebbing away and leaving behind swamps or stagnant pools" (2004: 205–206). This overwhelming expression of gloom is intended to be a challenge to have Cavell's readers prove him wrong, and to do so himself.

The greatest danger that true individuals face is captured by Nietzsche in his description of the Pale Criminal, an image he used to represent:

> the fate of human action as marking the actor with the unbearable consequences of his own striking out at, or into, the world. As though doing anything remarkable enough to be noticed as your action, one that is to be laid at your door, is risking becoming identified as nothing more than the doer of just that deed—not merely what you are but who you are is an adulteress, an informer, a draft dodger, a shoplifter, an unfit mother, a God-denier, a terrorist—put otherwise, the deed absorbs the power of your subjectivity. (2004: 240)

This happened, of course, to Nietzsche himself, whose pronouncement that "God is dead" got him labeled as a God denier for the rest of his life. But he was willing to take that chance, as any distinctive individual must be.

Later, in *Contesting Tears*, Cavell expressed his hope that Nietzsche would have liked the remarriage genre:

> Yet I rather fancy that Nietzsche would have seen the point of the comedies of remarriage, that he leaves it open to the future that a philosopher—granted that his or her marriage belongs in comedy—might be realizable as plighting a troth with someone who also sees the humor of the situation, that the sharing of laughter between friends is an increase not only of laughter but of philosophy . . . (1996b: 160)

In an essay "Psychoanalysis and Cinema," Cavell went much further:

> Nietzsche explicitly invokes the concept of marriage in his prophetic cry (in *Thus Spoke Zarathustra*) for this redemption or reconception of time. He says that it is 'high time' for this, and in German the literal translation of "high time" is *hochzeit* (wedding). Moreover, his symbol of eternal recurrence is the (wedding) ring. (Cavell 1996h: 225)

Like Emerson (and Cavell), Nietzsche was always an enthusiastic proponent of the values of laughter and friendship, which help us get over the overwhelming guilt and regret that results from the ascetic ideal. Significantly, Nietzsche's philosophy is at the heart of the "moral" that Cavell draws from the comedies of remarriage. Recall that the change that the couple must minimally undergo in order to reunite involves giving up seeking revenge against the other for his or her shortcomings and disappointments. Cavell interprets the significance of the genre as follows: "A comic No to marriage is farce, I am taking our films to be proposing a comic Yes. Nietzsche's vision of becoming a child and overcoming revenge is tied up with a new vision of time, or a new stance toward it, an acceptance of the Eternal Recurrence" (1981: 261—more on this in the following chapter).

The accepting attitude that Nietzsche urges us to adopt to the idea of Eternal Recurrence also helps Cavell explain the uniquely affirmative power of the comedies of remarriage: "The title registers, to my mind, the two most impressive affirmations known to me of the task of human experience, the acceptance of human relationship as the acceptance of repetition [in the sense of] Kierkegaard's study called 'Repetition', which is a study of the possibility of marriage, and Nietzsche's Eternal Return" (2004: 241). The fact that the separated couple freely chooses to reunite in the end reaffirms their love and devotion to one another in a way that the depiction of an idyllic relationship with no difficulties to contend with simply could not.

In *Contesting Tears*, this willingness to repeat one's life as it has been thus far is rightly seen as crucial to Nietzsche's enterprise: "the willing acceptance of repetition, or rather eternal recurrence, is the recipe Nietzsche discovered as the antidote for the otherwise fated future of nihilism" (1996b: 82–83). Cavell prefers characterizing his project as the overcoming of skepticism: "One can take the question of philosophy as the question . . . whether by my life I can and do affirm my existence in a world among others, or whether I deny this . . . It is some such question that Nietzsche took as the issue of what he called nihilism, . . . I persist, as indicated, in calling the issue by its, or its ancestor's, older name of skepticism" (1996b: 94). So, skepticism about the value of romantic love threatens to deny its value, and skepticism about all possible sources of value amounts to nihilism, if left unaddressed.

Near the end of his introduction to *Contesting Tears*, Cavell refers to Nietzsche's most infamous passages from *The Gay Science*, where the madman declares that God is dead, and that we have killed him. He sees this as analogous to the situation of the protagonist of the melodramas when she comes to the end of her trials: "The concluding position of the woman in the unknown woman melodramas . . . might perhaps usefully be studied in conjunction with that parable" (1996b: 43). Similarly, the unknown woman has typically become known by rejecting someone who held god-like power over her, someone whose domination of her earlier life had robbed her of a voice.

The unknown women in the melodramas, and the ex-wives in the remarriage comedies, are to be congratulated for undertaking the search for who they are:

> I find myself coming back to the opening question of Emerson's "Experience"—"Where do we find ourselves?"—which I take as emblematic of a perfectionist quest for orientation, responded to as such by Nietzsche, explicitly in the second sentence of *The Genealogy of Morals*: "How should we find ourselves since we have never sought ourselves?" (1996b: 374)

This takes courage, and a willingness to confront aspects of yourself of which you are far from proud.

Nietzsche was as critical of organized religion as Emerson or Thoreau. It is one of the major social institutions that enforce conformity, on pain of the loss of your soul. One of my favorite passages from Cavell in that regard is the following: "But Nietzsche persists in turning up an image of God as that of a riddled, bloody corpse whose open wounds we attempt to fill, i.e. deny with knots of religion, which is to say, with fragments of Christian suffering, especially guilt (Zarathustra 'On Priests')" (Cavell 1979b: 399). Both the comedies and the melodramas feature female protagonists who become nonconformists, enabling them to engage in the process of defining themselves in their own terms (and there is little talk of religion in either genre). One of Cavell's favorite examples is *Now, Voyager*, as a depiction of "the realization of the idea that Emerson and Nietzsche each phrase (not independently) as the courage to become who you are. This possibility, not alone of beauty, is the source of the film's glamour" (1996b: 122). The pursuit of Emersonian perfectionism demands revolt against societal norms, for only by becoming who they are can idealistic individuals make progress toward that "unattained but attainable self" at which they aim.

Cavell offered further evidence of the influence Emerson had on Nietzsche: "*Beyond Good and Evil* speaks, as Emerson does, of thinking through pessimism to affirmation. Nietzsche specifies pessimism as what is most world-denying; Emerson's name for this . . . is skepticism; its opposite Nietzsche specifies as world-affirmation, which is precisely what Emerson understands the new world to be awaiting" (2004: 199). Nietzsche was deeply concerned about the rise of what he called passive nihilism [naysaying for its own sake], as was Cavell (under another name). He had several brilliant insights into why "The Wasteland Grows," on one of the most interesting of which Cavell remarks: "I think this is something Nietzsche means, at the end of *The Genealogy of Morals*, when he speaks of man's being unable to empty himself of purpose and so finding a solution in taking emptiness as his purpose" (Cavell 1996i: 389).

Nihilism threatens because conformity reigns supreme, and few can manage to become who they are: "It obviously has precursors in Romantic perceptions of the human as dead or deadened, and it is a specific conceptual precursor of Nietzsche's 'last man' [who contemplates the collapse of human meaning and merely blinks in indifference], hence of Heidegger's *Das Man* [the they-self]" (Cavell 2005f: 128). The response to nihilism (or skepticism, if you prefer) is somewhat different in the two thinkers as well: "Nietzsche specifies the world-affirming human being as one who, reconceiving time, achieves the will to eternal recurrence; Emerson as one who finds the knack of liberation in moments" (2005f: 122).

When both call for "philosophers of the future," they are "explicit in saying that philosophy as such is thinking for the future – so that their sense of going beyond philosophy [as it has been thus far] in what they say about the future is at the same time a claim to the stance of philosophy" (2005f: 123). The future belongs to the visionaries who maintain a child-like sense of wonder. In *Pursuits of Happiness*, Cavell alludes to Nietzsche's famous description of the three metamorphoses of the spirit in *Thus Spoke Zarathustra*. In his view, we all start out as camels, beasts of burden who shoulder the responsibilities drummed into us by our parents. Then most of us become lions (in adolescence), saying No to those values. Finally (ideally), we create values of our own.

If they reach Nietzsche's creative, Yes-saying stage of the child, philosophers are visionaries, making new sense of existence, and articulating that sense in rhetorically effective (often poetic) terms. The lion stage that precedes it is "An expression of disgust with or disdain for the present state of things so complete as to require not merely reform, but a call for a transformation of things, and before all a transformation of the self" (1981: 262). The lion says No so the child can say Yes. This is what Nietzsche called active nihilism, which shatters all the "idols of the marketplace" in order to clear the way for new affirmations. It is then that Cavell uses Nietzsche to get at the essence of his comedies: "A comic No to marriage is farce. I take our films to be proposing a comic Yes" (ibid.).

In *Cities of Words*, Cavell praises Nietzsche for acknowledging Emerson's influence, and defends him against a misinterpretation by John Rawls of the implications of his notion of the Overman. Rawls took Nietzsche to be the archetype of a moral teleologist, who believed that the greater proportion of the resources of any society should be dedicated to its most outstanding members. As Cavell rightly points out, the question for Nietzsche is not one of distributive justice, but of who should lead society: "contrasting living 'for' the rare one with living for the many . . . you are already imitating one or the other of these . . . so your initiating task is to find one to follow from whom you can learn what it is to follow an idea on your own behalf, to find the one you are" (2004: 202).

In "Schopenhauer as Educator," Nietzsche admitted that we often need help in doing so: "Taking certain persons as exemplars to be emulated means that acting for their good or gain is acting on the basis of what you take as their idea or conception of good" (2004: 202). But, eventually, we must formulate our own conception of what is good, and cease being mere followers, in order to become the unique individuals (i.e. random mutations) that natural selection can operate on to promote the species.

For both Emerson and Nietzsche, "the present culture of society is the enemy of culture as it is called for" (2004: 203). The nineteenth century was an age dominated by moralists, and they are both disgusted by what "amounts to an impression of a perfect state of moralism, a stultification of individual and social freedom and originality" (2004: 204). Cavell proposes a "counter-reading of Nietzsche against the impulse to take him as an elitist indifferent to justice. 'The philosophical genius' is not a person with a particular talent or virtuosity but names a spirit in which life may be lived, dangerously, perhaps self-destructively . . . [a life of] freedom and again freedom" (2004: 206). That freedom is inevitably opposed by "what [George Bernard] Shaw calls the middle class and its morality [and] what Nietzsche called philistinism, borrowing from what Emerson called conformity" (2004: 396).

They also share a vivid awareness of the significance of the words that we say: "for Emerson and Nietzsche freedom, originality, in our thinking depends upon our speaking not merely in conformity with words, but for the sake, as if to achieve their meaning, of our words" (2004: 204). A new way of being requires a new manner of speaking, and of living accordingly (a theme that was developed at length by Martin Heidegger).

Other than their opposing attitudes to a transcendent metaphysical realm, the main difference between Emerson and Nietzsche is over whether self-reliance is a living option only for the few, or one that is open to the masses. As Cavell notes in the Introduction to *Cities of Words*: "Whether the perfectionist view that will emerge is essentially elitist, or on the contrary whether its imagination of justice is essential to the aspiration of a democratic society, is a guiding question of this book" (2004: 14). It is clear by its concluding essay that Cavell sides with Emerson on this issue, and embraces the democratic alternative that self-reliance is open to anyone willing to pay the price of nonconformity.

Nietzsche, on the other hand, held out little hope for the herd ever attaining autonomy. In his view, the majority will always conform eventually, just as the pseudo-hippies of the late 1960s became the Yuppies of the 1980s. *Übermenschlchkeit* (literally, "what it is like to be an Overman") can, by definition, only be attained by the few, and they should shepherd the herd with an eye to the future.

But these towering thinkers are alike in more ways than they are different. Cavell notes how "Often a sentence in Nietzsche's text is a recasting, through Nietzsche's temperament, of a sentence of Emerson's" (2004: 194). He offered a concrete example: "When Nietzsche says 'being truthful means: to believe in an existence that cannot be denied,' I hear Emerson in 'Self-Reliance' calling upon us to speak with necessity" (2004: 196). They also asked many of the same questions: "[Nietzsche] attractively uses the idea of man's 'metaphysical disposition' as his demand to answer the question 'What is existence worth as such?' 'Do you affirm this existence in the depths of your heart?' That is a question that Emerson was equally determined to raise" (ibid.). They both sought to sustain that affirmation throughout the course of their entire lives.

Despite the transcendentalism of Emerson and the atheism of Nietzsche, they are of one voice in calling for a radical transformation of their respective nineteenth-century societies. Cavell sees them as kindred spirits in their diagnosis of what is wrong as well: "Nietzsche's suggestion that it is not God's death that caused churches to turn into mausoleums, but the other way around, that our behavior in these habitations unsuits them for divinity—precisely Emerson's point when he speaks, half a century earlier, of preachers speaking as if God is dead" (Cavell 2005j: 257).

Above all, "the originality, or genuineness, or true humanity, these perfectionists demand of human existence requires a reconception and achievement of a genuine future, one not merely a continuation of the outworn past" (2005j: 197). This is why philosophy should be so controversial, and why the philosopher should be a tireless cultural critic, laying bare the hollowness of the traditional values of the culture:

> So the one claiming the life of philosophy, always groundlessly, is rightly reproachable for disturbing the peace. But he is right too . . . because the laws and the life of the laws, in any era, demand criticism, because our society and its culture—if it has justly won our consent to be governed by it—is not what it calls upon itself to be. (2005j: 207)

All of this funnels directly into Cavell's account of the two cinematic sub-genres on which he focused. In both, female protagonists are searching for new ways of making sense of their lives, by breaking free of conventional expectations, and finding the means to adequately express that sense. The works of film art he discusses make a similar statement: "I think of it as an attestation that there is perpetually a further possibility of ourselves, which it is the task of the genuine educator to encourage us to find. It is at the same time a demand for the further possibility of culture, call it the provision of the means of expression" (2005j: 200). Since life has whatever sense we can make of it, and whatever meaning we can infuse into it, this project of becoming who we are is of preeminent importance.

To return to Cavell's remarks in *Pursuits of Happiness*, the call to become who you are is issued against the backdrop of a cynicism shared by Emerson and Nietzsche about "the conventional masses as 'bugs, spawn', as a 'mob'. Nietzsche will say (something Emerson also says) 'herd.'" Cavell then asks the key question: "How do we, as Emerson puts it 'come out' of that? How do we become self-reliant?" (1981: 144). Well, first of all, we must turn away from the culture of today: "Emerson's word for being in contradiction with his today is his definition of thinking as being 'averse to the demand for conformity'. Nietzsche also explicitly in this matter evokes the notion of turning . . . challenging his reader to a 'reversal of one's estimations and esteemed habits'" (Cavell 2005a: 117).

Even Nietzsche's theory of the Will to Power finds its correlate at the end of Emerson's highly personal essay "Experience": "never mind the ridicule, never mind the defeat; up again, old heart!— it seems to say,—there is victory yet . . . and the true romance which the world exists to realize, will be the transformation of genius into practical power" (Emerson: 102). This is, of course, what Nietzsche envisions his resolute Overman to be, and do.

Cavell hears "echoes of Emerson" when Nietzsche speaks, in *Human, All Too Human* (1878) "of perspective (Emerson says partiality), and of our growing upward as a matter . . . of climbing the rungs of a ladder (Emerson says we find ourselves on a series of stairs), of being heard poorly (Emerson says being misunderstood)" (2005a: 119). He found Nietzsche to be almost as exciting, and life affirming, as Emerson: "The promise of Emerson and of Nietzsche is that youth is not alone a phase of individual development but—like childhood for the early romantics—a dimension of human existence as such" (2005a: 149). To be young at heart is to be open to transformative change, and this is the condition of all of the central couples in the comedies of remarriage, and of the unknown women in the melodramas.

These latter women are unknown because they have been robbed of their voices, by repressive husbands, or monstrous mothers, or callous lovers, who refused to hear them. Hence, they had to get beyond the need for a romantic or familial other to help them become who they were. Despairing of ever finding their romantic equal, they fashion their identities outside of marriage. In doing so, they follow Nietzsche's lead; he also gave up the search for romantic love. Nietzsche was a confirmed bachelor; he never lived with a woman who was not a family member, and had little good to say about women or romance.

Cavell argued that movies like *Now, Voyager* are liberating for women, not regressive (as many feminist critics have contended). In this connection, allow me to analyze one of my favorite films about a woman, Jane Campion's *The Piano* (1993), which, like the comedies of remarriage, has also generated strongly contrasting readings. My interpretation of its protagonist, a truly independent and unconventional individualist named Ada (Holly Hunter), will see her through the prism of Emersonian perfectionism and Nietzschean striving for one's "Higher Self."

Ada and her illegitimate daughter Flora (Anna Paquin) are shown to be decidedly unhappy in the mother country of Scotland. So she has resolved to become a mail-order bride, marrying a landowner named Stewart (Sam Neill) and moving to colonial New Zealand in the 1850s. She arrives on a rugged coastline with extensive personal belongings, and her piano. We learn from her interior voice (vocalized by Paquin) that she stopped speaking at age six, and hasn't uttered a word since, which might be taken as an early sign of her steely will, or of her traumatic early childhood. Stewart fails to ingratiate himself with her (as he would have done if he had considered himself a suitor) by insisting they cannot cart her piano inland, despite her entreaties to leave the rest of her stuff behind and bring the piano instead.

Along on the expedition is a man named Baines (Harvey Keitel), who is particularly intrigued by Ada. She comes to him begging to be taken to her piano, and when he sees how much she loves it he hatches a plan. Baines goes to Stewart and proposes that he will buy the piano, on the condition that Ada give him lessons. Stewart is always looking for money to purchase more Maori land, so he agrees, and when Ada protests, he demands that everyone must make sacrifices for the good of the whole. His assertion of selfish control alienates Ada from him completely, and her looks of anger and disdain are withering.

But despite her written insistence that the piano "is mine," she has little choice but to accept the arrangement.

Baines has the piano brought to his primitive shack, and has it tuned. Ada arrives and insists that she cannot teach him on a piano that needs tuning, and is pleasantly surprised when he has already done so. Baines changes the terms of the original arrangement, saying that he would rather simply listen to her play than take awkward lessons himself. Puzzled, she proceeds to play.

Soon his real motives become clear. When her daughter steps out of the shack for a moment, he bends and kisses Ada's neck. At first she is flabbergasted at his advances, but soon she enters into a negotiation with him. He tells her she can earn back the piano by granting him certain liberties, one key per visit. She says only the black keys should count, cutting her perspective favors in half. But he agrees, and Baines gets bolder and bolder with his advances as she plays.

Finally, in a testament to his nobility, Baines himself terminates their agreement, protesting his discomfort at reducing her to a whore. He gives her piano back to her long before she would have earned it, telling her of his hopes that she could love him. She is touched by this gesture, and returns to make love to him. What follows is one of the most tenderly erotic scenes in the history of cinema.

The liberation of women requires more than just granting them the freedom to act like a man. To my mind, images of women are most progressive when they depict traits that are generally considered to be feminine as virtues in their own right. *The Piano* is a film where the power of the female protagonist comes in large measure from her physical sensitivity. It is a supremely tactile film, which shows Ada to be in touch with the smooth keys of the piano, the soft cheeks of her daughter, the caresses of Baines, the buttocks of Stewart, and the enveloping silence of the ocean. She feels all of these deeply, and we do as well.

Ada is supremely her own person. Striking contrasts are drawn between her and the females in Stewart's home, who are like giggling schoolgirls. They remain indoors, sheltered against the harsh conditions that surround them. Ada simply does not conform to the conventions of Victorian womanhood, and revels in violating them. Her having a child out of wedlock, and venturing thousands of miles as a pioneer woman in a primitive colony, demonstrates her courageous nature. Even after having sex with Baines, she confounds our expectations.

One might think that Ada was prepared to leave Stewart behind her at this point. But she seems genuinely curious about whether a relationship with him is salvageable, which in turn depends on whether she can get him over his controlling nature. She comes into his bedroom and starts caressing him sensually, though refusing to let him touch her in the process. She explores this possibility for a while, until he shrinks from her decisively when she starts touching his buttocks and genitals. He is a lost cause.

Stewart goes off to fence some of his land, and gets her to promise she will not see Baines again (having surmised there is something between them). She removes one of her piano's keys and writes to Baines of her undying love, asking Flora to take it to him. But Flora has developed a loyalty to Stewart, and takes the key to him instead. Incensed, he rushes over to Baines' dwelling and sees them making passionate love through a crack in the wall. When she returns to his house, Stewart cuts off the index finger of her right hand and sends it to Baines, telling him there will be more to follow if he ever tries to see Ada again.

Through all this, Ada's self-possession remains complete. She utters no sound when he mutilates her, simply settling into the mud in her extreme pain. She refuses to be cowed by this ultimate gesture of domination, showing him no fear in her unmitigated disdain and disgust. Stewart finally relents, and Ada and Baines depart for civilization. But Ada is not through with surprising us.

The piano destabilizes the canoe the Maoris are using to take them to their ship, and one of the natives warns of the dangers of capsizing. Ada insists, over Baines' objections that she will regret it, on having them throw the piano overboard, noting that it has been tainted by recent events. When they do so, she puts her ankle into a coil of rope attached to it, and is dragged with it into the depths of the ocean. At the last minute, she chooses life and uncoils the rope from around her foot. She rises from the deep, and the film ends with idyllic scenes of the happiness of the three of them having founded a family in the old country.

This coda suggests that she was never as stoical as she acted, and that her oppression by a male-dominated society had taken its toll. But she chose life, and I believe it was because she had become who she wanted to be, and found the acknowledgment that Cavell valued so much from Baines. Cavell had also noted that his remarriage women have to go through some metaphorical type of death before reemerging as they truly are, with their own voice. Ada's interior voice puts her reflections on this experience this way: "What a death. What a chance. What a surprise! My will has chosen life. Still, it has had me spooked, and many others besides."[1]

As well as embodying the quest for Emersonian perfectionism (and Thoreau's notion of self-reliance), Ada can be seen as attaining the "Higher Self" of which Nietzsche spoke. In *Beyond Good and Evil* he characterized his "higher men" as having a particularly strong sense of the Will to Power: "Physiologists should think before putting down the instinct of self-preservation as the cardinal instinct of an organic being. A living thing seeks above all to discharge its strength—life itself is will to power—self-preservation is only one of the indirect and most frequent results" (Nietzsche, n.d.: section 13).

Throughout *The Piano*, Ada finds various ways to discharge her strength, in all three senses of power that Nietzsche proposed as his theory of value.

The Will to Power functions as a theory of psychological motivation. Nietzsche contends that people benefit others or hurt others from the same motive: to increase their own feeling of power, which Nietzsche believes to be the key to human happiness. This explains the seeming paradox in his contention that his Overman will be generous, and will seek to increase the power of those he leads. He does so for the sake of the feeling it gives him, and there is nothing more unambiguously pleasant than benefiting others by increasing their personal sense of power.

As a theory of value, the Will to Power has three facets. Having undercut traditional standards of valuation, Nietzsche must propose others or become a passive nihilist, who accepts the meaninglessness of existence. The measures of progress he proposes for the human race involve increasing the power of individuals in three senses: (1) control over self, i.e. achieving the individual autonomy that is necessary to command yourself to follow the values you choose; (2) control over the environment, to transform it to fulfill human desires; and (3) control of superior individuals over the herd majority. Ada is decidedly in control in all three senses of the term.

According to Nietzsche, most people will never be anything more than herd animals. Incapable of commanding, they must be told what to do, and they will do as they are told. Nietzsche designates the personality type that should be in control of society as the Overman, and in *Thus Spoke Zarathustra* makes it clear that only such individuals can redeem the human race from nihilism and allow it to better adapt to a rapidly changing environment. Nothing less than the future of the human species is at stake. A person who will be viewed by Nietzsche as an Overman is likely to be an artist, who uses a Dionysian way of thinking and feeling to create works that embody that individual's picture or interpretation of the world. Her values may or may not be the same as others ascribe to, but a good artist should be able to combine creativity with her perception of the world and life and express it in her work.

The vision of the Overman that he describes is not a timeless ideal for Nietzsche, but rather his personal notion of what the next progressive stage in human development should be. Let me apply the traits of the *Übermensch* (as identified by Harold Alderman in his wonderful little book *Nietzsche's Gift*, 1977) to better understand Ada's significance as a dramatic character who conveys a healthy and powerful image of women.

The *Übermensch* is someone who (1) expresses anger directly, and is (2) creative; (3) self-directed; (4) this-worldly; (5) self-aware; (6) proud (not vain); (7) egoistic; (8) experimental; (9) aristocratic; (10) discreet (masked); and (11) resolute. Well, Ada certainly expressed her anger directly, despite her aphonia. Signing and writing her responses, and embodying her feelings clearly in her facial expressions, she often displays the outrage that she understandably feels at attempts to reduce her to the traditional submissive Victorian bride. Her music sounds like nothing being played in the 1850s, and seems purely improvisational. She is decidedly self-directed; I believe she would have died rather than submit to the tyranny of her husband. She makes no reference to faith in God or an afterlife, and she seems to understand who she is and where she is going to a greater and greater extent as the film goes on.

For Nietzsche, the noble soul has reverence for itself. Ada is clearly proud, in the virtuous sense of evidencing a reasonable and well-grounded sense of self-respect. Unlike vanity, which seeks recognition from others, such respect depends only on one's own evaluation of oneself. Ada will not broach being disrespected by anyone, even her child. She is also egoistic; when she throws herself overboard, she shows little concern for Baines or Flora.

As her agreement with Baines and dalliance with Stewart demonstrate, she is willing to experiment to find what is right for her. She masks her power with her aphonia, yet clearly thinks herself superior to her female Victorian counterparts, and to the men who love her. She gets her piano back, and, once she decides that Baines is the one for her, she resolutely resists her husband until he frees her from their loveless marriage. She is unambiguously the most powerful character in the narrative.

Having demonstrated Ada's status as Overman, let me conclude by speculating about whether Nietzsche would have shared in the celebration of such liberation. I believe that Nietzsche might have welcomed true liberation for such unique women . . . after all, the love of his life was Lou Andreas-Salome, a highly unconventional thinker, psychoanalyst, and eventual commentator on his work. Unfortunately, Nietzsche had nothing directly to say about Cavell's favorite dramatic illustration of such liberation, Nora in Ibsen's *A Doll's House*. But I can't imagine Nietzsche would decry Nora's walking away from a marriage that wasn't worthy of the name, or condemn Charlotte Vale for keeping the love of her life at arm's length when she recognizes he is not her equal. Both are strong and proud, and have found their respective voices. Most inspiring to me is Charlotte in *Now, Voyager*, who, having given up (or at least suspended) the search for a romantic equal, fends for herself quite admirably.

Only liberated women can make relationships between equals of the opposite sex possible. It is that prospect that the remarriage comedies celebrate, which goes hand in hand with the notion that these couples are the best of friends, because they know one another better than anyone else, through the conversations they alone have shared. Recognizing the importance of that prospect should lead more men to welcome women's liberation out of sheer self-interest, as well as the increased hope for human flourishing. Baines does so, and is rewarded with Ada's love.

Two quotes from a chapter in *Human, All Too Human* indicate Nietzsche's sympathies in these matters. First, from section 377: "The perfect woman is a higher type of human than the perfect man, and also something much rarer. The natural science of animals offers a means to demonstrate the probability of this tenet." This seems to express a surprisingly liberated attitude, given the misogynistic tone of many of his remarks on women.

Nietzsche's potential approval of Cavell's project in *Pursuits of Happiness* is clearly signaled in section 406, which is entitled "Marriage as a Long Conversation": "When entering a marriage, one should ask the question: do you think you will be able to have good conversations with this woman right into old age? Everything else in marriage is transitory, but most of the time in interaction is spent in conversation." This consideration is even more important when one is considering remarriage, and is crucial to the decision of each of Cavell's couples to reunite.

In conclusion, what I have tried to do in this chapter is to demonstrate that Emerson, Nietzsche and Cavell are true intellectual soul mates, who are after very much the same thing in their respective philosophical projects. They are all equally convinced that a necessary condition for human happiness is to become who you are, and that doing so requires us (to use Emerson's phrase) to develop a powerful aversion to conformity, and a willingness to undertake the supremely difficult task of finding adequate means to express ourselves. Part of "The Good of Film" (to borrow the title of one of Cavell's essays) is that movies can, at their best, help us to do both. Films that serve to help liberate women, like the remarriage comedies, the melodramas of the unknown woman, and *The Piano*, are particularly effective in doing so.

NOTE

1. For *The Piano*, see https://www.springfieldspringfield.co.uk/movie_script.php?movie=piano-the (accessed November 3, 2018).

CHAPTER 5

Comedies of Remarriage and the Transfiguration of the Commonplace

Figure 5.1

... my investment in understanding the Hollywood comedy of remarriage is based in the claim that the central pairs in them are achieving, desire the achieving more than anything else, a structure of relationship that seems intuitively to satisfy the features of moral perfectionism—in their willingness and capacity for mutual education, for transformation,

Figure 5.2

for conversation, intellectual adventure, improvisation, devotedness . . . and for presenting, and being the cause of presenting, in unpredictable circumstances, the lineaments of satisfied desires, let's say happiness. (Cavell 1996b: 116)

Pursuits of Happiness: The Hollywood Comedy of Remarriage is Stanley Cavell's *Poetics*, a genre treatise that helps define his philosophy of film, and of life. These comedies relate the myth of the truly happy marriage, restoring our faith in the possibility, and inspiring us to practice Emersomian perfectionism ourselves. The typical plot of Cavell's favorite genre begins with a formerly married couple who are either about to be, or are already, divorced (in the films Cavell includes where the couple is not married to begin with, their romance is going anything but smoothly):

So marriage has its disappointment . . . and the disappointment seeks revenge, a revenge, as it were, for having made one discover one's incompleteness . . . Upon separation the woman tries a regressive tack, usually that of accepting as husband a simpler, or mere, father-substitute, even one who brings along his own mother. This is psychologically an effort to put her desire, awakened by the original man, back to sleep . . . (Cavell 1981: 31–32)

They have divorced because of some kind of serious difficulty, which has given rise to a desire to get out on the part of one or both parties in the couple.

Both are aggrieved, and they hold their separation against each other. They are going through a rough time: "I have identified the moment as located and inhabited by the remarriage comedies as one in which moral cynicism threatens, the temptation to give up on a life more coherent and admirable than seems affordable after the compromises of adulthood come to obscure the promise and dreams of youth" (Cavell 2004: 5).

But this does not lead to their complete estrangement. They seek out each other's company after the split, though often the women have become romantically involved with clearly unsuitable men in the meantime. The original couple circles around each other in a manner that makes obvious their continued attraction. Their ongoing conversations are electrically charged, and full of a vitality that is lacking in their verbal exchanges with others. They often include a lengthy lecture by the man to the woman, which is designed to help her become who she is. They reunite, less in the hope that they will radically change and more in the acceptance of who they are, both singly and together. Forgiveness is often asked for and granted, which is the only necessary major change. Their willingness to reunite, eyes wide open, has the power to affirm the validity of marriage and its ability to sustain ongoing romance, perhaps more than any other cinematic genre.

It gains this power because:

> nothing legitimizes or ratifies marriage [like] the willingness for reaffirmation, which is to say, for remarriage . . . and what makes marriage worth reaffirming is a diurnal devotedness that requires friendship, play, surprise and mutual education, all manifested in the pair's mode of conversing with each other (not just in words), which expresses an intimacy and understanding often incomprehensible to the rest of the depicted world, but which constitutes the truth of marriage. (Cavell 2005a: 121–122)

Pursuits of Happiness analyzes a series of classic Hollywood comedies from *The Lady Eve* to *The Awful Truth*, which embody the development of his concept of the genre in increasingly fuller detail. They contain some of the most witty, thoughtful and revealing conversations between the main characters in the history of Hollywood. Further, "it begins to emerge that these films are investigations of (parts of a conversation about) ideas of conversation, and investigations of what it is to have an interest in your own experience" (1981: 7). That interest is not just in fulfilling one's present desires, but in determining what they ought to be: "Put otherwise, the achievement of human happiness requires not the perennial and fuller satisfactions of our needs as they stand but the examination and transformation of these needs" (1981: 4–5).

Cavell addresses the defining characteristics of the genre in relation to *It Happened One Night*:

> Our films may be understood as parables of a phase in the development of consciousness where the struggle is for the reciprocity or equality of consciousness, between a woman and a man, a study of the conditions under which this fight for recognition (as Hegel put it) or demand for acknowledgment (as I have put it) is a struggle for mutual freedom, especially of the view that each holds of the other. (1981: 17–18)

This is a great deal of significance to invest in so-called "Screwball" comedies.

Continuing in the same serious vein, Cavell contends that "The conversation of what I call the genre of remarriage is . . . of a sort that leads to acknowledgment; to the reconciliation of a genuine forgiveness; a reconciliation so profound as to require the metamorphosis of death and revival, the achievement of a new perspective on existence" (1981: 19). This notion of having achieved a mutual acknowledgment through their revealing conversations is at the heart of Cavell's account.

The kind of acknowledgment Cavell had in mind says to the other that "You matter, perhaps more than anyone else." It must be reaffirmed continually, to overcome the threat of boredom at the prospect of the repetitions that inevitably come with marriage. It must be anchored in meaningful conversations that, as Cavell sees it, make who you are with far more important than what you are doing. Their exchanges with one another, on the fly or at length, are so entertaining because they are so true, and so revealing of who they are.

It is no coincidence that these comedies of the 1930s and 1940s begin with divorce, because it was a consideration that had become socially acceptable in post–World War I America. That made it a viable option for the first time in what, up until then, had been a painfully Puritanical culture. The comedies that Cavell loves make powerful statements against divorce, often by demonstrating that the decision to go their separate ways was, at best, rash and immature. In his view, these films serve to reassure the audience's growing skepticism about the ongoing validity of marriage, and the intimacy on which good marriages are based. Psychologists and marriage counselors have since concluded that the key to any successful marriage is communication. These films adamantly agree.

There is a good deal of drama in these comedies:

> The drama of the remarriage genre, the argument that brings into play the intellectual and emotional bravery of the beautiful, lucid pairs whose interactions or conversations form the interest of the genre . . . turns on their efforts to transform an intimacy between brother and sister into

an erotic friendship capable of withstanding, and returning, the gaze of legitimate civilization. They conduct, in short, the argument of marriage. (Cavell 1996h: 223–224)

Though Cavell himself gives the palm to *The Awful Truth*, I believe the epitome of this genre to be *The Philadelphia Story*. C. K. Dexter Haven (Cary Grant) and Tracy Lord (Katherine Hepburn) begin the film at each other's throats, with Tracy throwing out his golf clubs after breaking a couple, and Dexter pushing her down by her face. Their divorce goes unsaid (and unrepresented), and we cut to two years later, with Tracy preparing to marry a social climbing business tycoon by the name of George Kittridge (John Howard). Dexter crashes their wedding, showing up some time before it is scheduled to happen, to see if he can head it off. To further disrupt the pending festivities, he brings two reporters from *Spy* magazine to surreptitiously cover the event.

Their reasons for breaking up were serious. Dexter was an alcoholic, drowning his disappointment in his marriage in an ocean of drink. Tracy is still a critical perfectionist at the beginning of the film, and was a scold about his drinking, rather than giving him the support he needed to get on the wagon. Their divorce led Dexter to quit drinking, but Tracy still needs to get down off her high horse and forgive both herself and others for their inevitable shortcomings. Dexter is there to make one last attempt at dragging her off of it, before she marries a man who is absolutely wrong for her.

The formerly married couple carries on a vigorous dialog throughout the film, which reveals that they were clearly meant for each other. They share the social graces of old money that the social climbing fiancé lacks, and an enthusiasm for sailing that he cannot appreciate. In the course of their exchanges, Dexter seeks to educate Tracy about her superior attitude, as much for her sake as for his own.

Dexter isn't the only one to lecture her on humility ... her father, ostracized for his affair with a Broadway starlet, also urges her to come down off her high horse, and to be more forgiving. She heeds his advice after she gets drunk on champagne and puts herself in a compromising position with journalist Macauley ("Mike") Connor (James Stewart), who refuses to take advantage of her intoxicated state. She finds that she must lower her priggish standards in order to better forgive herself, as well as Dexter and her father. As Dexter puts it, "Oh, how the mighty have fallen!"

Cavell observes that:

Comic resolutions require the acquisition in time of self-knowledge, say, as a matter of learning who you are ... the form this education takes in them is her subjection to fits of lecturing by the men in her life ... The women of our films listen to their lectures because they know they need to learn something further about themselves, or rather to undergo some change, or creation . . . (1996h: 56)

Dexter's initial diatribe is withering, and goes to the heart of his frustration with her:

> It's astonishing what money can do for people, don't you agree, Mr. Connor? Not too much, you know. Just more than enough. Take Tracy, for example. There was never a blow that hasn't been softened for her . . . she's a girl who's generous to a fault. To a fault, Mr. Connor. Except to other people's faults. For instance, she never had any understanding . . . of my deep and gorgeous thirst . . . You took on that problem with me when you took me, Red. You were no helpmate there.[1]

Turning to Mike, he continues: "strength is her religion, Mr. Connor. She finds human imperfection unforgivable. When I discovered that my relationship to her . . . was supposed to be not that of a loving husband and a good companion but . . . that of a kind of high priest, to a virgin goddess, then my drinks grew deeper and more frequent." Rather than helping him overcome his drinking habit, her nagging had simply made it worse.

Despite their troubles, Dexter still loves her:

> Red, you could be the finest woman on this earth. I'm contemptuous of something inside you you either can't help or won't try to. Your so-called "strength" . . . your prejudice against weakness, your blank intolerance . . . Because you'll never be a first-class human being or a first-class woman . . . until you've learned to have regard for human frailty. It's a pity your own foot can't slip a little sometime . . .

But Tracy isn't ready to hear him just yet.

George seems to confirm Dexter's characterization of her as a goddess: "You're like some marvelous, distant, well, queen, I guess. You're so cool and fine and always so much your own. There's a kind of beautiful purity about you, Tracy, like a statue." But that is not what Tracy wants to hear: "I don't want to be worshipped. I want to be loved." She does not want to be flattered by being called a goddess; she seeks to be praised for who she is.

Then her father blames his infidelity (in part) on her:

> What most wives fail to realize is that their husbands' philandering . . . has nothing whatever to do with them.

-Oh? Then what has it to do with?

–A reluctance to grow old, I think. I suppose the best mainstay a man can have as he gets along in years . . . is a daughter. The right kind of daughter. I'm talking seriously about something I've thought over thoroughly. I've had to. A devoted young girl gives a man the illusion . . . that youth is still his.

–Very important, I suppose.

–Oh, very, very.

Because, without her, he might be inclined to go in search of his youth. That's just as important to him as it is to any woman. But with a girl of his own, full of warmth for him . . . full of foolish, unquestioning, uncritical affection . . .

–None of which I've got.

He then reaches the crux of the matter:

–You have a good mind, a pretty face . . . a disciplined body that does what you tell it. You have everything it takes to make a lovely woman except the one essential. An understanding heart. Without that, you might as well be made of bronze.

–That's an awful thing to say to anyone.

Yes, it is indeed. Tracy's reaction makes it clear that his words have struck home.

At this point, another romantic rival for Tracy's affections enters the scene. Macauley Connor (played by Jimmy Stewart, in an Oscar-winning performance), had written a book she thought highly of, and she offers to be his literary patron (he refuses). Later, she violates her sober-minded principles: for only the second time in her life, Tracy gets drunk, and is seemingly swept off her feet by Mike.

At first they squabble about nothing, then Tracy confirms that her father's lecture took hold by aiming the same criticisms at Connor: "You're so much thought and so little feeling, Professor . . . Your intolerance infuriates me! I should think that, of all people, a writer would need tolerance. That fact is you'll never, you can't be . . . a first-rate writer or a first-rate human being . . . until you've learned to have some small regard for human fra—" She trails off at the end of the word "frailty," as she becomes aware she is echoing her father's sentiments.

Connor turns on the romantic charm, praising her virtues as a human being: "You're lit from within, Tracy. You've got fires banked down in you . . . hearth fires and holocausts!—I don't seem to you made of bronze? No. You're made out of flesh and blood. That's the blank, unholy surprise of it. You're the golden girl, Tracy . . . full of life and warmth and delight." They then decide to go for a moonlight swim. Though the situation gave him ample opportunity, Connor refuses to take advantage of her ("there are rules about that"), and carries her nearly limp body back to the house. So now she has three men to choose from, two of whom possess real merit.

Dexter talks with Liz, and asks her why she hasn't married Macauley yet:

-You really want to know?

-Mm-hmm.

-He's still got a lot to learn. I don't want to get in his way for a while.

-It's risky though, Liz. Suppose another girl came along in the meantime?

-I'd scratch her eyes out, I guess. That is, unless she was going to marry somebody else the next day.

Liz is the most mature and even handed of all the characters.

Hung over on the morning of her wedding, Tracy expresses some serious self-doubts (while reflecting on the nature of true conversation): "Oh, Dext! I'm such an unholy mess of a girl. That's no good. That's not even conversation. But never in my life . . . not if I live to be a hundred . . . will I ever forget how you tried to stand me on my feet again today." She recognizes him as a true friend. When Dexter tells her he is thinking of selling their sailboat, the *True Love*, and building another boat called the *True Love II*, her outraged response expresses her continuing love for him for the first time:

-If you call any boat that, I promise I'll blow you and it out of the water. I'll tell you what you can call her . . . In fond remembrance of me . . . the *Easy Virtue*.

-Shut up, Red. I can't have you thinking things like that about yourself.

-What am I supposed to think when I . . . I don't know. I don't know anything anymore.

-That sounds very hopeful, Red. That sounds fine.

They have reached the brink of reconciliation. But first Dexter's romantic rivals have to be ruled out.

George is pretty easily disposed of. In an indignant letter to her, he made the distrustful assumption that Tracy and Mike had had sex. When this is disconfirmed, George tries to justify his mistrust "A man expects his wife to behave herself. Naturally." This stands in stark contrast with Dexter's preference for a wife "[t]o behave herself naturally," i.e. to be who she is by doing what she feels like. This is the last in a series of repressive gestures, which she succeeds in throwing off: "George's idea is always to constrict her behavior, as when he responds to her wish to be useful by saying that instead he is going to build her an ivory tower; and as when at the party, in response to her tipsy gaiety, he disapprovingly insists that it's time for them to leave. He in effect takes himself out of the running" (2004: 28). Finally recognizing George's crass conventionality, Tracy dismisses the prospect of marriage to him with a withering remark: 'I'd make you most unhappy. Most. That is, I'd do my best to."

She has more trouble rejecting Mike's last-minute proposal: "Why not? Because I don't think Liz would like it . . . and I'm not sure you would . . . and I'm even a little doubtful about myself. But I am beholden to you, Mike. I'm most beholden." This is the only instance in the genre that I know of where the woman has to make a choice between two men of merit. Generally, she jilts someone who is dead wrong for her, in favor of her former husband. To my mind, introducing Conner, who, for once, is an attractive alternative, serves further to confirm that Tracy and Dexter were made for each other.

Why does she (re)choose Dexter now? Tracy acknowledges him "as another to [her] separateness [granting him] what Emerson calls 'the recognition that he exists' . . . Hence Tracy learns, or has learned, that Dexter is ready, that he is her company, that they exist. It is what she expresses to her father by declaring her feeling that she is a human being" (2004: 29).

The connection between him being both her best friend and the one she loves is natural:

> Marriage is an allegory in these films of what philosophers since Aristotle have thought about under the title of friendship, what it is that gives value to personal relations, and this is a signature topic of perfectionism . . . life . . . is a weave of cares and commitments in which one is bound to become lost and to need the friendly and credible words of others in order to find one's way, in which at any time a choice may present itself . . . in pondering which you will have to decide whose view of you is most valuable to you. (2004: 15)

Dexter has, throughout the film, expressed respect, love and admiration for Tracy, despite her faults, and she chooses him because his view of her is most valuable to her, as her best friend.

She insists on announcing to the wedding guests that her marriage to Kittridge is off, not knowing quite what she will say, but adamant that "Whatever it is, I'll say it. I won't be gotten out of anything anymore, thanks." At a loss about how to proceed after announcing she won't be marrying George, she enthusiastically repeats Dexter's promptings "Three years ago I did you out of a wedding in this house by eloping.—Which was very bad manners. I'll make it up to you by going through with it now as originally planned."

Their exchange after the public announcement is telling:

Tracy: Are you sure?
Dexter: No, but I'll risk it. Will you?
Tracy: You bet. You didn't do it to soften the blow? Nor to save my face?
Dexter: No, it's a nice face.
Tracy: I'll be yare now—I'll promise to be yare.
Dexter: Be whatever you like.

Both Tracy (who has come down off her pedestal) and Dexter (who has quit drinking and embraced himself) are now willing to accept themselves as they are, and not as they had expected each other to be.

Tracy immediately shares her joy with her father:

–Tracy, darling . . .

–I love you, Father.

–I love you too.

–Never in my life have I been so full of love before.

–Come along. Come along.

–Wait. How do I look?

–Like a queen. Like a goddess.

–And you know how I feel?

–How?

–Like a human. Like a human being.

The moral of the story is profound, though it has become a cliché: the only way to find happiness in marriage is to be yourself.

The confrontational plot dynamic of *The Philadelphia Story* (and the other remarriage comedies) is inherently philosophical, according to Cavell, because "the quarrel is going to have to take up questions about who is active and who is passive, and about who is awake, and about what happiness is and whether one can change." We quickly develop a rooting interest in seeing the divorced couple reunited: "The pair is attractive [and] their wishes are human, their happiness would make us happy. So it seems that a criterion is being proposed for the success or happiness of a society, namely that it is happy to the extent that it provides conditions that permit conversation of this character" (2004: 32).

The intent of these films was, for their time, pretty progressive: "I think of them, as a group, to be dedicated to the pursuit of what you might call equality between men and women (and of this as emblematic of the search for human community as such—but I am letting this pass for the present), the pursuit of their correct independence of, and dependence upon, one another" (1988: 16). Yet there is a serious asymmetry between the sexes as treated there that feminist critics have pointed out, and which Cavell acknowledges: "What the comedies of remarriage show is that, as the world goes, there is an unfairness or asymmetry in this pursuit, because women require an education for their assumption of equality, and this must be managed with the help of men. The first task for her, accordingly, is to choose the best man for this work" (ibid.).

But it is not just this unfairness and asymmetry that accounts for the hostility these women harbor in their hearts toward their men: "It is not fully explicit until the last of the definitive remarriage comedies, *Adam's Rib* in 1949, that what the woman has against the man is fundamentally the simple villainy of his being a man; hence that is what her happiness with him depends on her getting around to forgiving him for" (1988: 17). Tracy Lord shows this developing willingness to forgive in her remark after Mike reassured her that nothing had happened between them that drunken night: "I think that men are wonderful."

Cavell recognizes the extent to which the filmmakers are putting one over on us with their romantic myths: "Preston Sturges [in *The Lady Eve*] is trying to tell us that tales of romance are essentially feats of cony catching, of conning, of making gulls and suckers of their audience" (1988: 48). Perhaps where they con us the most is by encouraging our faith in the prospects for radical change in romantic relationships. Reconciliation is achieved believably in *The Philadelphia Story*. The aggrieved parties had to change to some extent, if they were to successfully reunite; at minimum, "this changing is the forgoing or forgetting of that past state and its impasse of vengefulness" (1988: 32). Tracy and

Dexter make the shift from obsessing about their past to looking to a future together.

One thing that smooths their reconciliation over is that Cary Grant was an actor "who . . . carried the holiday in his eye; who exhilarated the fancy by flinging wide the doors of a new mode of existence, who shook off the captivity of etiquette with happy spirited bearing, good natured and free as Robin Hood . . . if need be calm, serious, and fit to stand the gaze of millions" (1988: 43, quoting Emerson). George, and even Mike, never had a chance against him.

So, what does it all mean: "The overarching question of the comedies of remarriage is precisely the question of what constitutes a union that makes these two into one, what binds, you may say what sanctifies in marriage? When is marriage an honorable estate?" (1988: 53). The answer that *The Philadelphia Story* offers is that marriage only supports the search for self-realization when the couple love to be with one another, and have a great time doing so. This is alone made possible by the quality of their conversations, in which they reveal themselves to one another, and acknowledge their mutual love. This total acceptance of each other as they are, and can be, also involves "learning, or accepting, your sexual identity, the acknowledgment of desire" (1988: 56).

The Philadelphia Story shares another characteristic with members of this genre: "the absence of children further purifies the discussion of marriage. The direct implication is that while marriage may remain the authorization for having children, children are not an authentication of marriage" (1988: 58). Their absence also unmuddies the couple's divorce, morally speaking, as only affecting the two of them.

Rather than wanting to be parents, "[a]lmost without exception these films allow the principal pair to express the wish to be children again, or perhaps children together. In part this is a wish to make room for playfulness within the gravity of adulthood. In part it is a wish to be cared for first, and unconditionally" (1988: 60). This alludes to Nietzsche's observation that the key to a powerful life is to regain the seriousness of a child at play. It also provides a crucial affirmation that it is OK to pursue happiness, and that children still retain the most natural inclination to do so.

Continuing the thought, Cavell notes that what makes these comedies unique is not that they affirm the pursuit of happiness:

> It is not news for men to try, as Thoreau puts it, to walk in the direction of their dreams . . . to pursue happiness. Nor is it news that this will require a revolution of the social or of the individual constitution, or both. What is news is the acknowledgment that a woman might attempt this direction, even that a man and a woman might try it together and call that the conjugal. (1988: 65)

The genre is distinctive in its ability to affirm marriage as a true source of conjugal bliss.

But the makers of movies of remarriage do not pose as if they have all the answers: "The happiness in these comedies is honorable because they raise the right issues; they end in undermining and in madcap and in headaches because there is, as yet, no envisioned settlement of these issues" (1988: 65). One of the most major unsettled issues remains the question of whether change can be radical, and if it can last. Do these comedies celebrate the possibility of radical change? Not really: "Can human beings change? The humor, and the sadness, of remarriage comedies can be said to result from the fact that we have no good answer to that question" (1988: 259). Raising the question, however, is part of what makes these films so philosophical, and the myth that the films tell inspires faith in fundamental change nonetheless, a belief that makes it more likely that a person will change.

It is a testament to the breadth of his philosophical influences that Cavell's final characterization of the moral of this story is cast in terms drawn from the famed early section of Friedrich Nietzsche's *Thus Spoke Zarathustra*, entitled "On the Three Metamorphoses": "A comic no to marriage is farce, I am taking our films to be proposing a comic Yes. Nietzsche's vision of becoming a child and overcoming revenge is tied up with a new vision of time, or a new stance toward it, an acceptance of the Eternal Recurrence" (1988: 261).

As a test of whether one has attained Overman status, Nietzsche raised the prospect of an eternal recurrence, i.e. of living one's life over and over again exactly as one has thus far, to see how his readers would react. If you can say of your entire past "thus I will it so," you will relish the thought; those still burdened with regrets and harboring revenge in their hearts will dread the possibility. Tracy and Dexter have both reached the point of "Thus I will it so." The embrace of what makes them good together prepares them for accepting the inevitable repetition of some of their problems, despite their reconciliation. This type of film "in short, poses a question concerning the validation of the marriage, the reality of its bonding . . . the answer to that [question is] that the validity of marriage takes a willingness for repetition" (1988: 26).

Furthermore, "Dexter's demand to determine for himself what is truly important and what is not is a claim to the status of a philosopher" (1988: 150). Philosophical issues are being raised here, and what is at stake is nothing less than the identities of the major players.

But, as noted above, Cavell also acknowledges that a "moral cloud" hovers over the structure of these films. The fact that it is the woman who stands in need of education, and must find her educator in her romantic choice, who lectures her about her shortcomings, has more than a hint of sexism about it, which feminist critics have pointed out for years. He describes this "moral cloud" explicitly in a later book, *Contesting Tears: The Hollywood Melodrama of the Unknown Woman*, "Does creation from, even by, the man somehow entail creation for the man, say for his use and pleasure and pride. If not, how does the woman attain independence; how does she complete, as it were, her creation?" (1988: 116). He never answers this question directly, but simply admits "that the happiness achieved in remarriage comedy is not uncontaminated, not uncompromised" (ibid.). Yet he defended the genre as ultimately depicting the search for equality in a marriage.

Cavell captured the positive significance of these stories best in a comment from *Contesting Tears*:

> In remarriage comedy the transformation of the woman is accomplished in a mode of exchange or conversation that is surely among the glories of dialogue in the history of the art of talking pictures. The way these pairs talk together I propose as one perfect manifestation of what Milton calls that "meet and cheerful conversation" which he . . . took to constitute God's purpose in instituting sexual difference, and hence what is generally called marriage. (1988: 87)

This notion, that conversation is part of what makes life worth living, moves me to seek more meaningful conversations with my own significant other. Like so much of his work, Cavell's account of the remarriage comedies has a therapeutic effect on his readers.

That effect is perhaps best summarized in a piece on *North by Northwest*, where Cavell compares it to the remarriage comedies: "their goal is the thing I call the legitimization of marriage, the declaration that happiness is still to be won there, there or nowhere, and that America is a place, fictional no doubt, in which that happiness can be found" (Cavell 2005d: 55). What could be healthier for us to believe?

The last question to address here is "Why America?" Because "America is the name of the locale of the second chance, or it was meant to be. Remarriage is the central of the second chances" (Cavell 2005e: 97). America is a nation of immigrants, who came to this country looking for another chance at life. Like those immigrants, who made America what it is, the protagonists in these comedies find a second chance to be together, and seize it firmly, despite its insecurities.

Let me conclude with one clear example of the recurrence of Cavell's remarriage themes in contemporary romantic comedy, *Eternal Sunshine of the Spotless Mind* (2004), which is my favorite movie of the current millennium. Joel Barish (Jim Carrey) and Clementine Kruczynski (Kate Winslet) are an unlikely couple to begin with. After an undetermined amount of time together, Clementine decides to end the relationship definitively by erasing it from her memory, and Joel follows suit (but incompletely). Unbeknownst to us initially, the film begins when they meet again on a train. In the course of the film, they learn they were involved before for several months, when one of the employees of the memory-erasing company informs them of their alteration (of which only Joel had any recollection, however dim).

Joel and Clementine never got married in the first place, as many of their generation failed to do. But they were clearly in a significant relationship, considering that Clementine went to the trouble and expense of having it completely wiped from her consciousness. They know that they had real problems as a couple, though they cannot recall what those problems are, or how likely they are to recur. They have to decide whether to become intimate again, given these circumstances.

Joel bemoans the fact (to himself) that he is the kind of insecure guy who falls in love with any girl that shows him the least amount of attention. Clementine describes herself to him as someone whose goal "is to just let it flow through me . . . Do you know what I mean? It's like, there's all these emotions and ideas and they come quick and they change and they leave and they come back in a different form and I think we're all taught we should be consistent."[2] Despite their differences, they do talk well together, and she gives him her phone number and urges him to call her. He does, almost as soon as he gets back, and the relationship is on.

In their most charming moment, Clementine gets Joel out on a frozen bay at night, and they are seen lying down together in a striking overhead shot. Joel points out constellations, and she scoffs. Soon, Joel is crying outside her house, and the next thing we know the technicians from Lacuna Inc. are at his door to erase his memory. When their relationship ended she wiped him from her mind, literally, and Joel decided to follow suit. He has to collect everything in his possession that is associated with Clementine. They expose him to the memorabilia one by one, from which they draw a neurophysiological map of what areas of the brain need to be erased.

But he is resistant to the process from the first. Two guys invade his home with their equipment and hook him up to a scary-looking helmet. We see scenes as they are being erased, from his memory, including the couple's last night together, when she informs him that she wrecked his car while driving drunk. She accuses him of wondering whether she was out with someone else, while he assures her he assumed she had sex that night, because "isn't that how you get people to like you?" She stalks out, ending things, as the memory gets fuzzy and fades out.

The Lacuna team includes Patrick (Elijah Wood), who's already going out with Clementine, and Stan (Mark Ruffalo), who has the Lacuna receptionist Mary (Kirsten Dunst) come over to join them. They are drinking beer and thinking about sex, and not paying close attention to their delicate operation. Though he is supposed to be totally unconscious, Joel starts hearing them talk about Patrick and Clementine. Previous memories are erasing incompletely, and Joel overhears Patrick tell Stan that he is using Joel's notes on Clementine to seduce her.

As his memories gradually disappear, conflicts are uncovered, including her wanting a baby while he feels that they are not ready to do so. Mary arrives, starts drinking whiskey, and utters a significant Nietzsche quote for the first time: "Blessed are the forgetful, for they get the better even of their blunders." Another memory emerges, of Clementine bemoaning the fact that she tells him every embarrassing thing about herself, while he doesn't tell her much. His response is that "Constantly talking isn't necessarily communicating."

His mind is discombobulating at this point. He hears Patrick talking to Clementine on the phone while he is talking with her in a restaurant. Joel then sees her in the Barnes & Noble with him, while hearing that he is leaving Joel's apartment to comfort Clementine. A good flashback is wiped of his liking her newly colored orange hair, and of her admitting she thought she was ugly as a kid, while Stan and Mary smoke a joint and get totally wasted. She is enamored of their boss, Dr. Howard Mierzwiak (Tom Wilkinson), who invented the process.

Joel wants to retain that orange hair memory, and the one of them going out on the ice. But now it is during the day, and he tells Clementine he is happy and is just where he wants to be . . . only he is suddenly in Grand Central Station for a moment, then on the ice at night alone. His mind fragmenting before his very eyes, he decides at that point that he wants to call the memory wipe off. He is screaming, but Stan and Mary are drunkenly dancing in their underwear and pay no attention.

Memories flash by quickly now, and he grabs Clementine, telling her he thinks he knows how to stop it. He tries to go back to Mierzwiak and get the machine turned off, but he is still just inside his own head. Meanwhile, Patrick is using Clementine's memorabilia to seduce her, even saying the same things Joel said (and recorded in his journal). Joel manages to wake himself up for a moment, which affects the process. Stan and Mary wake up from making love to a buzzer indicating that the machine has stopped erasing. They call Mierzwiak in the middle of the night to get him out of bed and come down to Joel's apartment to bail them out. As Mierzwiak tries to boot the program back up, Joel is now thinking of his early childhood, and being bathed in the sink by his mother.

Joel wakes up again, and the doctor gives him a shot to knock him out. Mierzwiak gets the machine going and Joel loses another dear memory, of himself and Clementine watching a drive-in movie while providing the dialog themselves. But he has developed a resistance to the procedure, and is retaining fragments of memories. Mary shares the *Beyond Good and Evil* quote with Mierzwiak, who identifies it as Nietzsche immediately.

Joel loses another dear memory, of their seeing the elephants from the Barnum and Bailey circus on the streets of New York. Mary recites the central quote from Alexander Pope from which the title of the movie is taken ("How happy is the blameless vestal's lot! The world forgetting, by the world forgot. Eternal sunshine of the spotless mind! Each pray'r accepted, and each wish resign'd"), and kisses the good doctor. He protests that he is a married man, with children, but his wife pulls up and sees them through the picture window together. She says she expected this, and we wonder why. Then the wife alludes to Mary having had him before . . . they had already had an affair, which was wiped from Mary's memory at her insistence.

As his memories fade, Joel visits the Barnes & Noble in his mind and pleads with Clementine to give him another chance, and that it would be different. They meet again at a beach picnic party, and break into another beach house down the way. As it deconstructs along with his memory, he admits to Clementine that he ran away because he was scared. Cut to Stan turning the machine off and declaring the erasure to be complete.

At this point we cycle back to the opening scene, with Joel playing hooky and meeting Clementine on the train coming back from Montauk. Only this time when they stop by her apartment the next morning he waits for her rather than bolting like an anxious horse. As they drive away, Clementine opens a package from Lacuna. Dissatisfied with not knowing of her own alteration, Mary has decided to inform everyone who had their memories erased about the procedure, and Clem plays her tape of the negative things she said about Joel. He concludes that Clementine must be screwing with him and throws her out of the car. Patrick is waiting at her door when she gets back, but she drives him away.

Clementine goes over to Joel's place, and finds him listening to his tape from Lacuna. He now knows it's true, and that they had their memories of each other erased. He had a lot of hurtful things to say about her as well, so the tables are turned. She is chagrined at his embittered comments, and goes to leave. But he catches her in the hall and begs her to wait a moment: "Clem: I'm not a concept Joel, I'm just a fucked up girl looking for her own peace of mind. I'm not perfect. Joel: I can't see anything that I don't like about you. Clem: But you will. You will think of things, and I'll get bored with you, and feel trapped . . . because that's what happens with me. Joel: Okay (and she nods her head and says Okay too)." Then they laugh together. The film ends with them romping at the beachfront in the snow, to the following tune: "Change your heart, look around you. Change your heart. It will astound you. Now I need your loving, like the sunshine, And everybody's gotta learn some time." So, how did their hearts change, and what did they learn?

First, they learned to take their time and not run out on each other. Everybody has to learn that problems in a relationship are inevitable, and must be accepted as intermittently recurring. Their hearts forgave each other for all the cruel things they had said on the tape, a process that was made easier by the fact that they could not remember the incidents that gave rise to them. Most significantly, they acknowledged that Joel was demanding and finicky, and Clementine was easily bored and restless, and that they were okay with that being the case.

Eternal Sunshine of the Spotless Mind is my favorite postmodern romance, because their choice to reignite their romance involved accepting that whatever problems they had previously were likely to arise again. Not knowing what they were, the couple is more than likely have to deal with them again, with no previous experience to draw upon in order to avoid them. But at least there is no compulsion to change hanging over them, because they don't have any idea what changes might be called for, nor do they harbor unreal expectations of how much one can change for the sake of another.

They overcome the spirit of revenge, because they cannot recall anything for which they might want to avenge themselves. They don't have to forget the ways in which they hurt or disappointed each other the first time around, because they have already wiped the slate clean. This enables them to enjoy a truly fresh start. The feeling that the audience is left with is hopeful, even exhilarating, as they take another chance on love, able to do so because they have put their past behind them. What the original romantic couples in these remarriage comedies needed to metaphorically forget, their previous problems, Joel and Clementine had literally forgotten, which made it possible for them more easily to begin again.

Their willingness to do so is life affirming, and underscores the point of the song at the end that love is as nourishing as sunshine, and as necessary to lives like ours. Their joy at being together again gives us hope that romance is not merely a deceptive ephemera, but rather a wellspring of human meaning, well worth the suffering it inevitably causes. Forgetting the past allowed them to embrace what Nietzsche called the "Eternal Recurrence of the Same," the repetitions that are inevitable in any long-term relationship. This willingness to repeat is at the heart of the remarriage comedies, according to Cavell, and of *Eternal Sunshine of the Spotless Mind*.

NOTES

1. See https://www.springfieldspringfield.co.uk/movie_script.php?movie=philadelphia-story-the for all further quotes from *Philadelphia Story*.
2. For script of *Eternal Sunshine of the Spotless Mind*, see https://www.springfieldspringfield.co.uk/movie_script.php?movie=eternal-sunshine-of-the-spotless-mind (accessed February 19, 2019).

CHAPTER 6

How the Unknown Woman Finds her Voice in *Contesting Tears*

Figure 6.1

> The persistence of this feature of metamorphosis indicates the cause of these genres as among the great subjects of the medium of film, since a great property of the medium is its violent transfiguration of creatures of flesh and blood, its recreation of them, let us say, in projecting and screening them. (Cavell: 1996b: 7)

Figure 6.2

Almost fifteen years after the publication of *Pursuits of Happiness*, Cavell returned to genre theorizing (and creation) with his discovery of the Hollywood Melodrama of the Unknown Woman. He saw the two types of films as complementary: in the remarriage comedies, a woman finds self-realization within marriage, after a transformation brought about by conversations with her former spouse. In the melodramas, a mousy woman who has been viciously repressed by her mother, husband, or lover finds that she does not require a spouse to become who she is. Freeing herself from the repressive force, she finds her voice and speaks her mind, elbowing her way back into the conversation. Both genres are "marked by the suggestion that its principle puts herself in the way of a transfiguration or conversion of her life that I associate with the teachings of Emerson and Thoreau and that I claim to be common to the members both of the genre of remarriage and of the melodrama of the unknown woman" (1996b: 219).

Like the comedies of remarriage, the melodramas also represent a response to a form of skepticism. Since both address ordinary, everyday concerns about marriage, "then the threat to the ordinary called skepticism should show up in fiction's favorite threat to forms of marriage, namely, in forms of melodrama" (Cavell 1996c: 319). Comedies of remarriage show the unhappy couple coming to realize they are the best of friends, and repairing their relationship as a result. By contrast:

> In the set of melodramas studied in the present book, the woman's answer to that possibility of friendship is an unreserved no. Since it follows for her that she thereby says no to marriage as such, as presently conceived . . . it follows further that these melodramas bear an internal relation to the remarriage comedy. (1996b: 11)

In his readings of perennially popular melodramas in *Contesting Tears*, Cavell sought to define "a genre of film, taking the claim to mean, most generally, that they recount interacting versions of a story, a story or myth, that seems to present itself as a woman's search for a story, or of the right to tell that story" (1996b: 3). If our identities are determined primarily by the stories we tell ourselves about ourselves and others, earning the right to tell one's own story is a fundamental task in the process of successful self-definition.

The female protagonist of these melodramas must wrest that right away from the extremely dominant person who has robbed her of her voice. Her search for herself is different from the remarriage comedies: "The chief negation of these comedies by these melodramas is the negation of marriage itself—marriage in them is not necessarily reconceived and therewith provisionally confirmed, as in remarriage comedy, but rather marriage as a route to creation, to a new or original integrity, is transcended" (1996b: 6).

While the women in the remarriage comedies have found conversational equals worth embracing, the unknown women fail to do so: "the women are claiming the right to judge a world as second rate that enforces this sacrifice (of her selfhood); to refuse, transcend, its proposal of second rate sadness" (1996b: 127). Cavell provides a general template for his new genre: "Then the sense of character (or underlying story or myth) of film I was to look for . . . may be formulated in the following way: a woman achieves existence (or fails to) or establishes her right to the form of a metamorphosis (or fails to), apart from or beyond satisfaction by marriage" (1996b: 87–88). She makes "A certain choice of solitude (figured in a refusal of marriage) as a recognition that the terms of one's intelligibility are not welcome to others—at least not as the basis for romantic investment in any present other" (1996b: 12).

The mode of "existence" that she achieves requires the protagonist to live an autonomous life, and find her voice, while forgoing the need for a spouse. These women all have an ill-defined sense of self when their respective stories begin; for various reasons, they clearly lack self-esteem. Repressive forces of some kind "serve to isolate the woman of this melodrama from everyone around her . . . Hence I speak of the genre as a study of the unknownness of the woman" (1996b: 117). Someone is inside the shell the unknown woman hides within, but she has no voice; those who repress her have (both literally and figuratively) shut her up, and "This denial of voice is not the loss of speech . . . but a loss of reason, of mind as such—say the capacity to count, to make a difference" (1996b: 58).

The most terrifying example of this can be found in *Gaslight*, where "we are given the perfect contradiction of the education and creation sought in remarriage comedy; in this melodrama the woman is meant to be decreated, tortured out of her mind altogether" (1996b: 49). But Paula (Ingrid Bergman) breaks free of her husband's Svengali-like spell over her, and Cavell's account of how she does so reveals much about the genre he is discussing:

> [in a] full throated melodramatic climax of ironies, in which the woman confronts her husband alone—brandishing a knife with which she might free him or kill him . . . and delivers to him her *cogito ergo sum*, her proof of her existence which I might translate for this film roughly as "Now I exist because now I speak for myself; and in particular because I speak in hatred and to you . . . who I now know will alone understand my every word and gesture" (as if, in our mysterious world, to exist is to take revenge). I call this late moment Paula's aria, and its declaration causes, or is caused by . . . her metamorphosis or creation, which is what one should expect of the assertion of the *cogito* that, as in Descartes, puts an end to skeptical doubt. (1996b: 47–48)

There are many defining elements of the genre present here, so let me spend some time unpacking this very long quote.

Remember, in *Gaslight*, Paula's husband Gregory (Charles Boyer) is trying to convince her that she is insane. He does so, as Cavell puts it, by pretending to understand her, and not to understand her, at crucial junctures. This is the ultimate form of subjugation and repression of her individuality, and he succeeds in robbing her of her voice for most of the film. He has led Paula to doubt not just her sanity but her existence as an independent individual with a valuable perspective on life.

As in the comedies, the female protagonists in the melodramas are trying to find their own voices and become who they are. Just as the *cogito* answers skeptical doubts about one's very existence, the "arias" of the unknown women make them known to themselves, and their antagonists. Like Paula, Lisa Berndle (Joan Fontaine) in *Letter from an Unknown Woman* (1948), and Catherine Sloper in *The Heiress* (which I will add to the genre at the end of this chapter) hate the men who have shut them up and deceived them, and find their voices, in part, in order to revenge themselves on their oppressors.

Lisa writes her fatal letter after seeing Stefan Brand (Louis Jordan) years after her teenage infatuation with him, which led to an affair that resulted in her bearing his child. She is married now, to a man that loves her and raises the child as his own. But seeing Stefan again rekindles her one great passion in life. She seeks out his company, but he doesn't even remember who she is, and treats her as another of his many casual affairs. After this total failure of acknowledgment, her bitter missive begins with the line "By the time you read this letter I may be dead," from the fever that she mentions later on. Reading her letter, and being moved by it, leads Stefan to go through with a pending duel (i.e. pistols at dawn) that he had planned on ducking before receiving it. She does find her voice, but only at the end of her story, and of her life. The satisfaction we feel at his demise is different from what audiences enjoy at seeing Charlotte having come into her own, and gotten beyond all thoughts of revenge or resentment.

Cavell's reading of *Now, Voyager* is his most inspiring statement of the myth these films are supposed to tell. Charlotte Vale (Bette Davis) is not a vengeful person. She is a literal nobody when the film begins. Overpowered emotionally by a domineering mother who tells her what to wear, how to act, and how to keep out of the public eye, she is an overweight frump, who can neither speak for herself nor resist this maternal tyranny. On a cruise with her mother early in the film, a dashing young officer proposes; her mother forbids her to see the man, and that is that. She has no life of her own outside of her room.

But then she finds a sympathetic therapist in Dr. Jaquith (Claude Rains), director of the sanitarium where she takes up temporary residence: "In losing control early to Dr. Jaquith, Charlotte refers to herself as 'my mother's companion,' 'my mother's servant,' and the place she is first shown to live in . . . as 'her mother's room' . . . These are all names, I mean descriptions, carved in stone" (1996b: 142). They name her servility, her total submission to her mother's will.

After emerging from the sanitarium, and having been revived by Jaquith's insightful support, Charlotte goes on an unaccompanied cruise. This was an unconventional step for any single woman to take at the time, let alone one of questionable mental health. She dons an entirely new wardrobe (courtesy of an old female friend), complete with impeccably stylish hats, and steps outside of herself, breaking the bonds within which her mother had kept her tied. As early as *The World Viewed* (1971), Cavell remarked upon this scene: "merely to think of the way, in *Now, Voyager*, her restoration to sanity is signaled by an opening shot of her sheer-stockinged ankles and legs, released from the thick, shapeless, dark cotton wrappings and health shoes into which her wicked mother had charmed her—these moments provide us with a fair semblance of ecstasy" (Cavell 1971: 5–6).

Concerning her transformation, which involves taking on a new "look," Cavell later observes: "This does not read to me as some testimony to accepted beauty; but rather the contrary. It seems to me a realization of the idea Emerson and Nietzsche each phrase . . . as the courage to become the one you are" (1996b: 122). Charlotte always had it in her, but her mother hid her light under a bushel. It is no accident that the cover illustration for *Contesting Tears* is of the "new" Charlotte Vale, as she walks down the gangplank of the cruise ship in Rio.

Wearing a trim suit and stylish hat, she has lost a good deal of weight, and her face is made up in the latest fashion. She is trying on an alternate persona, which soon becomes a smash hit. Here the film announces emphatically that it is about her transformation. It "is preoccupied with change, a preoccupation laid on with a trowel . . . the camera (in the famous shot of her descending the gangway) moves from her feet up the length of her body to conclude on a gorgeous white hat, half shading a modeled face, an image of mystery, presaging adventure, heralding metamorphosis" (1996b: 119).

On her own, she is soon paired up with a married man named Jerry Durrance (Paul Henreid), whose wife could not come with him at the last moment due to ill health. They are immediately attracted to each other, share some adventures (including a car accident), and strike up a romantic relationship. They declare their mutual love, but Jerry is ultimately loyal to his spouse and child, and soon flies back home to be with them. In his absence, Charlotte becomes the social hit of the cruise, making new friends and enticing new suitors.

When she returns home, the "new" Charlotte exudes a palpable erotic energy: "From where does this erotic power proceed? . . . it comes from attention paid to her by men on the boat . . . beginning with attention from Jerry" (1996b: 120–121). When the mother seeks to reestablish dominance, by trying to again dictate what Charlotte wears, whom she sees and even what she eats, the daughter rebels, insisting on a new vision for her life, retaining her newfound style, and acting just as she pleases.

Charlotte meets a different man, and becomes his fiancée, but then rejects him after she sees Jerry again. The news that she has cancelled her engagement literally kills her mother, and Charlotte returns to the sanitarium, never to refer to the cause of her repression again. There, "She is spared [simply being cared for by Dr. Jaquith] by the discovery of the young girl —Jerry's daughter—which gives her a chance to recreate herself through saving, let us say, the child. It is a relation of creation that, however equivocal, in her world nothing called marriage can replace" (1996b: 146–147).

Charlotte finds meaning in her life by becoming the surrogate mother and lay therapist of a young woman who faced a similar degree of neglect, disdain and belittlement from her mother as Charlotte had from Mrs. Vale. This gives her a newfound sense of purpose. When Dr. Jaquith sees this, he remarks: "I thought you said you came here to have a nervous breakdown," to which she responds: "Afraid that I've decided not to have one." This shows how far she has progressed since her first visit to the sanitarium, when she had little choice but to undergo an emotional collapse.

By the kind of coincidence that happens only in Hollywood, Tina Durrance (Janis Wilson), the young girl Charlotte is helping, is Jerry's daughter. Mrs. Durrance has managed to make both her husband and daughter miserable. But when Jerry hears that Charlotte has taken Tina into her house, he is less than pleased. Despite seeing the healthy changes in his beloved daughter, he adopts a condescending attitude: "No self-respecting man would allow such sacrifice as yours to go on indefinitely." He then announces his intention to take Tina home. No more willing to submit to his emotional tyranny that she was to her mother's, Charlotte immediately puts him in his place: "That's the most conventional, pretentious, pious speech I ever heard in my life. I simply don't know you."

Finally receiving some much needed emotional recognition from a woman, Tina is becoming who she is, tracing the path from ugly duckling to swan that Charlotte had already traversed. What brought them out of their respective shells was receiving the genuine care and concern that had been denied them by their heartless mothers. In my most recent viewing, I was moved to tears by the scene where Charlotte presents a revitalized Tina to Jerry for his approval. He immediately registers the positive transformation she has brought about in his beloved daughter, and Charlotte beams when she sees how much it means to him. More than the melodramatic ending, Charlotte's ultimate gesture of autonomous caring was the emotional climax of the film. These so-called "women's pictures" still pack an emotional punch for me, in part because I used to watch them while growing up with my highly empathetic mother, who loved to tear up at the occasional "weepie."

Cavell rejects feminist critics who argue that *Now, Voyager* is a regressive tale, where Charlotte "sacrifices any new life of her own in favor of a sterile pact with Jerry to remain faithful to the memory of their hopeless love" (1996b: 227). He accuses them of underestimating her, just as Jerry did when he tried to forbid her from taking care of Tina, and proposes an alternate reading:

> we are shown that Charlotte perceives Jerry's destructive guilt to be about to cause further destruction, in the form of removing his daughter from Charlotte's protection and love, and shown further that he is incapable of responding to Charlotte in her assumption of her freedom and power. Accepting the fact that he has reached the limits of his powers of comprehension, she allows him to delude himself in peace. (1996b: 227)

Having recognized that their marriage would be inappropriate, Charlotte accepts what she can have: being of significant use in the sanitarium (and dedicating her home and her inheritance to expanding its facilities), cherishing the memory of their romantic fling, and the feeling that she and Jerry are raising June together.

Forever grateful for Jerry's love, which facilitated her self-realization, she is content to leave the romantic side of their relationship behind them. He has failed to measure up to her expectations, and has acquiesced to the life of convention. She has taken charge of her own life, given style to her own unique character, and left her mother (who apparently dies of what they used to call apoplexy when Charlotte refuses to marry) behind her, with no regrets.

By the end of the film, Charlotte has found a new way of being, by becoming a co-parent to Jerry's child, and a useful colleague of Dr. Jacquith. She can help other unknown women find their identities, because she appreciates what it is like to be unknown, in ways the good doctor never could. She has fashioned a meaningful life for herself outside of marriage, and wouldn't have it any other way. Charlotte Vale is a healthy role model for women, in Cavell's eyes, because she answers our doubts about whether a woman is capable of turning her life around.

Though she has the sense that she is now living a meaningful life, she should not be mistaken as having attained happiness. Remarking on how seldom she is shown smiling in the course of the film, and how much Jerry wanted to make her happy, Cavell observes that "her insistence on immunity to happiness suggests that what she is remains unrecognized, perhaps unrecognizable. (It seems reasonable to suppose that she will never come to the end of mourning for her life.)" (2004: 226). Those who long for a marriage between the two forget this, and that Dr. Jaquith was her psychoanalyst.

On the cruise, Charlotte calls herself by a different name. This is linked to her search for a voice of her own: "The story of *Now, Voyager* can be considered as a retelling of the fantasy of the ugly duckling. It is a recounting for grown-ups of the way a name . . . can make you ugly, that tells how hard it is for a human being to find the way to her or his (legitimate?) name, the name of the kind to which one is kin" (1996b: 141). Once she doffs her name (with the help of Jerry), she is on the road to recovering her sense of self. She comes to a broader realization as well: "that the various names and labels that have been applied to her (another pervasive theme of the film) are none of them who she is. That this is a desirable therapeutic result I would like to maintain from a philosophical point of view of what the self is, something which no set of predicates can in principle exhaust" (1996b: 227).

Realizing this permits Charlotte to embrace her own perspective, and to value it as the equal of anyone else's. Indeed, many of these melodramas are best understood as exercises in what Friedrich Nietzsche called "perspectivism," where the central conflict involves a struggle over whose interpretation shall win out in the woman's eyes:

> Melodrama, in its negations of communication, of what I call conversation, may be said to be about interpretation, about the fact that an interpretation, being a way of seeing or taking something, contains as part of its grammar (in Wittgenstein's way of speaking) that there is a competing way, a way this way eclipses . . . *Gaslight* . . . makes the competition of interpretation its explicit narrative theme, a man's effort to drive a woman mad by demonstrating to her that she is incapable of a voice in her self-interpretation. (1996b: 169)

Having a voice means expressing your perspective, i.e. describing how things look from your unique point of view.

Cavell's exemplars fit his formula with varying degrees of exactitude, with *Now, Voyager* to be taken as the archetype. In *Gaslight*, Paula is freed from her husband's clutches by Detective Cameron of Scotland Yard (who Cavell suggests plays the role of analyst). *Letter from an Unknown Woman* ends tragically with the deaths of the protagonist and of her tormentor/lover. It also departs from the genre in that "The failure to overcome revenge gives *Letter* a special place in the genre of the unknown woman . . . (it shows) in a rawer state, yet not less sophisticated, the magnitude of the forces arrayed against the woman's chances of exercising her judgment" (1996b: 178).

Cavell's account of *Stella Dallas* has allowed me to see it in a totally different light. Feminist critics have long accused the film of being retrograde in its depiction of a mother sacrificing everything else about which she cares for the sake of her daughter's social success. I tended to see it that way until Cavell's interpretation triggered a gestalt shift in my understanding of the ending. In his view, the feminist critics are like Jerry in *Now, Voyager*: they think of Stella's act in purely conventional terms, while Cavell contends that she is actually engaged in freeing herself from the forces of social conformity. The accepted reading has it that Stella continues to desire the acknowledgment of the upper crust throughout the film. This is why her sacrifice is so great, for by its end she has forsaken any chance she had of gaining that acceptance. This interpretation underestimates Stella and overestimates the extent of her self-sacrifice. Cavell makes a pretty compelling case for seeing Stella as having turned her back on social climbing, when she turns away from the window through which she is observing her daughter's wedding celebration and walks straight into the camera at the end.

Crucial to his case is the scene where Stella wears an outrageous Christmas tree of an outfit, apparently trying to "fit in" with the elite class with which her daughter is now socializing. This mistaken reading "is based on the assumption that Stella at the resort hotel is 'as oblivious as ever to the shocking effect of her appearance' when she makes a 'Christmas tree' spectacle of herself. My thought is that the pressure of this interpretation is excessive, too insistent, that there is massive evidence in the film that Stella must know exactly what her effect is there" (1996b: 255).

Her embarrassing costume is traditionally seen as a sincere attempt to impress that fails, confirming that Stella simply doesn't have the class to move in such circles. Cavell suggests rather that "there is massive evidence in the film that Stella knows exactly what her effect is there, that her spectacle is part of her strategy for separating Laurel from her . . . The evidence . . . turns simply on her massively authenticated knowledge (of clothes), that she is an expert at their construction, and, if you like, deconstruction" (1996b: 201).

Suddenly, a social failure to be pitied turns into a brilliant maneuver to be admired, for "her spectacle is therefore part of a strategy for traumatically separating Laurel from her, not a catastrophe of misunderstanding that causes her afterward to form her strategy" (1996b: 255). By this point in the film, "Stella learns the futility of appealing to the taste of those who have no taste for her . . . It is this learning—on the way of looking at things I am following—that precipitates the scandal in the resort hotel in which Stella appeals, as it were, to the distaste of those for whom she knows she is distasteful" (1996b: 202)

Cavell summarizes his radical reinterpretation: "What I have called the accepted view . . . takes Stella to accept her own barring from that world . . . still convinced of its incalculable desirability . . . my opposed view takes Stella to learn that the world Laurel apparently desires—of law, church, exclusiveness, belonging—is not to her taste" (1996b: 211–212). So Stella should be seen as having liberated herself from the forces of conformity, while facilitating her daughter's choice to conform.

Seeing her as freeing herself from social expectations in order to become who she is puts her story in the realm of Emersonian perfectionism. Cavell believes "that Stella has the right not to share their tastes, that she is free to leave not just the man of the marriage but the consequences of a marriage she allowed herself to believe would transform her" (1996b: 217). Henceforth, she will seek to flourish without a spouse, and with a daughter who is no longer her highest priority. So, Emerson's philosophy offers us a new way of seeing Stella as taking charge of her life, rather than giving it up.

In defense of the value of doing the philosophy of film, Cavell contends that both benefit from their rather unlikely amalgam:

> The acceptance of such an idea (of the woman's transfiguration) would provide a certain verification of this philosophy, hence of philosophy as such, as I care about it. To propose the idea may be seen as part of my effort to preserve that philosophy, or rather to show that it is preserved,

is in existence, in effect, in works of lasting public power—world famous, world flavored films . . . (1996b: 220)

Seeing these films from the point of view of Emerson's philosophy helps infuse them with a greater intellectual seriousness than they had hitherto possessed, while seeing Emerson's philosophy as realized in these films serves to validate its continuing relevance to the modern age. *Now, Voyager* is the clearest example of the bunch of the self-realization that Emerson was talking about.

Contesting Tears discusses fewer melodramas (four) than *Pursuits of Happiness* does comedies (seven). In order to explore the genre and its connection to the theme of vengeance further, I will conclude this chapter with my own original interpretation of *The Heiress*, another unknown woman melodrama from Hollywood's golden age. It opens by introducing us to Dr. Austin Sloper (Ralph Richardson), who is discussing his daughter Catherine (Olivia DeHavilland) with his sister Lavinia (Miriam Hopkins). He inquires whether she is beginning a new embroidery, and when informed she is, makes the first of a number of disparaging remarks about her: "I hope she doesn't let it become a life's work." He then asks Lavinia to extend her visit in order to "help Catherine" to join in with the young people at a forthcoming party and forge a social life outside the home. Even before seeing Catherine, we know she is the daughter of a condescending and judgmental father.

In one of her introductory scenes, we learn that she is a wallflower with little or no self-confidence in her ultimate worth. Lavinia pleads with her not to go off on her own at the wedding reception, as she usually does:

Catherine: You have been talking to Father.
Lavinia: Well, yes, dear. In a way I have. Your father . . .
Catherine: Father would like me to be composed, and to join in the conversation.
Lavinia: Yes.
Catherine: I can't, Aunt Lavinia.
Lavinia: Perhaps you don't try sufficiently.
Catherine: Oh, I do! I do! I would do anything to please him. There's nothing that means more to me. I have sat here in my room and made notes of the things I should say and how I should say them. But when I am in company, it seems that no one wants to listen to me.[1]

Like Charlotte by her mother, Catherine is dominated by a disapproving father that she would do anything to please. She has no public voice, perhaps because her father does not respect anything she might say.

Dr. Sloper reveals his true feelings about his daughter to an acquaintance at the party:

She's gone to the best schools in the city, she's had the finest training I could get her, music and dancing. She's sat with me evenings on end. I've tried to make conversation, give her some social adeptness. I've given her freedom wherever I could. The result is what you see. An entirely mediocre and defenseless creature with not a shred of poise.
Liz: Austin, you're so intolerant. You expect so much.
-You remember her mother, Liz? Her mother who had so much grace and gaiety. This is her child.
-Austin, no child could compete with this image you have of her mother. You've idealized that poor dead woman beyond all recognition.
-You are not entitled to say that. Only I know what I lost when she died. What I got in her place . . .

Initially, Catherine does not fare very well at the party. The first man to dance with her goes off with another woman while she is waiting for him to bring her back some punch. Mortified, she is on her own again.

Then her aunt introduces her to Mr. Morris Townsend (Montgomery Clift), and things start looking up. They dance, and he actually returns afterword with drinks for them both, only to find her dancing with an older man (who "ambushed" her with Aunt Lavinia's approval). Undeterred, Townsend arranges to call on Catherine the next day. This leads to a whirlwind courtship that leaves Catherine breathless. After she returns from a walk that consciously kept Townsend waiting for some time after their appointment, he sings a song to her that clearly foreshadows the fate of their relationship:

> Townsend: Can you hear me way over there? You know, on my tenth visit, you might even sit here.
> Catherine: Mr. Townsend, you are very bold. (He sings the song.)
> Townsend: Do you know what it means?
> Catherine: No.
> Townsend: The joys . . . of love . . . they last . . . but a short time. The pains . . . of love . . . last all your life. All . . . your life. It's a lovely song. You know, I think of you constantly.

Their romance soon begins to take flight. Yet even with Townsend, she still struggles to find her voice:

> Townsend: I think you talk very well.
> Catherine: Not when I need it most. Oh, with Miss Penniman, or in my room at home I can think of the most delightful things to say. Can you understand that?
> Townsend: Yes, I can.

> Catherine: But here with you, I sound like a fool.
> Townsend: I don't think so.
> Catherine: You don't? Well, if ever you do think so, if ever I sound high-blown or false, put it down to that, will you?
> Townsend: I will try.
> Catherine: And . . . take pity on my situation.
> Townsend: What situation? Miss Sloper . . . I have fallen in love with you.
> Catherine: You have?

How could she resist such apparent acceptance from him?

The first interview of Townsend by Dr. Sloper does not go well. It seems that Townsend has no job, and had been living on a small inheritance that is now used up. He says he seeks a position, but has no idea of what it might be. Townsend senses the doctor's suspicion of his motives, which is confirmed when Sloper speaks to Lavinia:

> Lavinia: He's so agreeable. So elegant.
> Sloper: He may find it hard to maintain elegance without working for it.
> Lavinia: But he's looking for a position earnestly.
> Sloper: I wonder if he's looking for it here, Lavinia. Wouldn't being husband to a defenseless girl with a large fortune suit him to perfection?
> Lavinia: How can you entertain suspicion?
> Sloper: Suspicion? It's a diagnosis, dear.

The stage is set for a confrontation. Anticipating such a blow up, Townsend addresses his anxieties:

> Townsend: Your Aunt, she's on my side. She wouldn't let your father abuse me.
> Catherine: My father won't abuse you. He doesn't know you well enough.
> Townsend: You know . . . I would've liked you to say to me, "My father doesn't think well of you, what does it matter?"
> Catherine: But it would matter. I could never say that.

He then proposes, and she accepts. But Townsend knows there are problems ahead, the biggest one of which is his lack of money and her $30,000 a year.

Before having the crucial meeting with Townsend, who will ask for Catherine's hand in marriage, Sloper consults with the young man's sister. Though reticent to say anything against him, she informs the doctor that he went through his inheritance quickly, spending it on himself:

> Mrs. Montgomery: He told me that he'd used up a small inheritance.
> Sloper: Did he handle it well?

Mrs. Montgomery: Probably you would not think so. But from his own point of view, he did a great deal with it. He saw Europe. He met many interesting people. He enlarged his capacities.
Sloper: Did he help you, ma'am?
Mrs. Montgomery: No.
Sloper: Shouldn't he have?
Mrs. Montgomery: I don't think so.
Sloper: You are a widow and have children. I think so.

He then points out that Townsend still wears the finest clothes, while her wardrobe is somewhat shabby. Nonetheless, his loyal sister refuses to complain about him, telling Sloper: "I think, Doctor, you expect too much of people. If you do, you'll always be disappointed." But the good doctor is adamant: "consider how he has behaved with money. He gratified his every wish. Did he help you with the children? No! He enlarged his capacities in Europe. He left his gloves here last night, the finest chamois. Look at yours. Will he help you with this fortune he hopes to marry? I would stake my life he would not!" Needless to say, when Townsend asks for Catherine's hand, her father refuses.

Townsend is hesitant to marry Catherine without her father's consent, so they agree that she should go on the six-month trip to Europe her father insists on to see how enduring their feelings are for each other. But she refuses to give him up, not yielding one inch to her father's entreaties, and they return early from their travels. The following climactic exchange finally frees Catherine from his clutches:

Sloper: Well, I suppose you'll be going off with him any time now.
Catherine: Yes, if he will have me.
Sloper: Why not? You'll be a most entertaining companion.
Catherine: I will try to be.
Sloper: Your gaiety and brilliance will make up the difference between the 10,000 a year you will have and the 30,000 he expects.
Catherine: He expects nothing. He does not love me for that.
Sloper: No? What else, then? Your grace, your charm, your quick tongue and subtle wit?
Catherine: He admires me.
Sloper: I've tried for months not to be unkind. But now it's time for you to realize the truth. How many girls do you think he might have had in this town?
Catherine: He finds me pleasing.
Sloper: Oh, yes, I'm sure he does. A hundred women are prettier, a thousand more clever. But you have one virtue that outshines them all.
Catherine: What? What is that?

> Sloper: Your money!
> Catherine: Father!
> Sloper: You have nothing else!
> Catherine: Oh. What a terrible thing to say to me.

Freed from her dutiful feelings toward her father by his disrespect and disdain for her, she consents to an elopement against his wishes. He had spoken to her as if he despised her, and something snaps within her at such cruelty.

The lovers breathlessly make arrangements for him to return for her in two hours. But, in their discussion of the ramifications of this decision, Catherine makes it clear that her father will disinherit her, and that, in her opinion, there are no prospects for reconciliation. In his disappointment at this news, he abandons her, and borrows enough money to travel to California and seek his fortune.

This leads to a final confrontation with her father:

> Sloper: You are flushed. Your eyes look sick. You have been weeping. You have broken your engagement. Oh, if you have, I must tell you, Catherine, that I admire you greatly for it. I know the effort you must have made.
> Catherine: Do you, Father?
> Sloper: But in time the pain will pass. I cannot begin to tell you how proud of you I am.
> Catherine: Are you?
> Sloper: Oh, deeply. Most deeply proud.
> Catherine: He deserted me.
> Sloper: What?
> Catherine: Morris deserted me. Now do you admire me, Father?
> Sloper: Oh, Catherine.
> Catherine: Don't be kind to me. It doesn't become you.
> Sloper: Are you blaming me because I tried to protect you?
> Catherine: Yes.
> Sloper: Someday you will realize I have done you a great service.
> Catherine: I can tell you now what you have done. You have cheated me. You thought any handsome, clever man would be as bored with me as you were. It was not love that made you protect me, it was contempt.
> Sloper: Morris Townsend did not love you, Catherine.
> Catherine: I know that now, thanks to you.
> Sloper: Better to know it now than 20 years hence.
> Catherine: Why? I lived with you for 20 years before I found out you didn't love me. Morris may not have hurt me or starved me of affection more than you did. Since you couldn't love me, you should have let someone else try.

Sloper: You have found a tongue at last, Catherine. If only to say such terrible things to me.
Catherine: Yes. This is a field where you will not compare me to my mother.

This last line demonstrates her understanding of the basis of his indifference to her, an unfair comparison with his sainted wife, to whom no one could have measured up.

Catherine has finally found her voice, not because of the recognition from Townsend, but because her father's dominance of her has been ended by his callousness. He starts to compose a new will that disinherits her, but (like Charlotte's mother) is overcome by the onset of an illness that will prove fatal. Cavell notes this as another characteristic of the genre: "Does Charlotte cause her mother's death? Parents sometimes create the impression that claiming one's own existence will mean the end of theirs. We might say that the birth of freedom may require taking such a chance" (1996b: 141). Like Charlotte, Catherine shows little concern for his demise. Her transformation from mousy doormat to powerful individual is now complete.

Some years later, Mr. Townsend returns to New York, and Catherine's aunt arranges for her to see him. Having failed to make his fortune, he had returned from California to plead his case:

Townsend: Now that I'm here, you will give me the chance to vindicate myself. You must hear me out, Catherine. You must. For the sake of what we have been to each other.
Catherine: What is it you want to explain?
Townsend: Many things, Catherine. May we not sit down now? Catherine, it was because I loved you that I disappeared that night. I know how it looked. I behaved abominably. But I knew that if I returned that night, I might have done you great harm. No man who really loves a woman could ever permit her to give up a great inheritance just for him. It's only in storybooks.
Catherine: My father did not disinherit me, Morris. He threatened it to test you.
Townsend: But I couldn't be sure of that the night . . . I went away.

Apparently moved by his plea, Catherine consents to run off that night and get married. But she will not be fooled twice by the same man: "He came back with the same lies. The same silly phrases. . . . He has grown greedier with the years. The first time he only wanted my money, now he wants my love, too. Well, he came to the wrong house, and he came twice. I shall see that he never comes a third time." When her aunt asks her if she can be so cruel, she responds: "Yes, I can be very cruel. I have been taught by masters. Right here."

The film ends with Mr. Townsend getting his comeuppance. He appears before her house with a carriage at the appointed time, but she bars the door to him, and he is left to plead with her in vain to open it. She gets her sweet revenge, having freed herself from both of her oppressors. Unlike Charlotte, however, there is little sense of who she will become in their absence. She has given up embroidery, and has nothing in its place. She lives in the family house on Washington Square, leading what may still be a totally isolated existence. Perhaps this is why Cavell did not include *The Heiress* among the exemplars he discussed in his book, although it fits the pattern so well otherwise.

I definitely had a very different response to the end of *The Heiress* than I did to the conclusion of *Now, Voyager*. Revenge is sweet for Catherine Sloper, but, as noted, her transformation does not seem to have led to a satisfying independent life on her own. Lisa Berndle welcomes the idea of death at the end of her tale, and Paula looks likely to develop a new romantic relationship with the detective who helped extricate her from her plight by reassuring her of her sanity. By contrast, Charlotte Vale has put her mother behind her, and wishes only the best for Jerry Dorrance, despite rejecting him as a romantic prospect because of his conventional narrow-mindedness. This is what makes her story the epitome of the melodrama of the unknown woman.

According to Cavell's reading of *Stella Dallas*, Stella is more like Charlotte than like Catherine Sloper. She harbors no grudge against the high society that rejected her, because she no longer values the class in question. These women foster a healthier image of independence, for I would argue (following Nietzsche) that acting to revenge yourself against another is a sign that they still hold power over you that you resent. Both Charlotte and Stella had freed themselves from that resentment, and are focused on fashioning a future life of their own.

NOTE

1. For script of *The Heiress*, see https://www.scripts.com/script/the_heiress_9797 (accessed February 28, 2019).

CHAPTER 7

Cavell and Wittgenstein on Skepticism: Redeeming the Law

Figure 7.1

Stanley Cavell has long championed my favorite thesis on what the movies do best. As I once put it in an article for the *Film-Philosophy* online journal: "the movies are magical according to Cavell because they embody myths, which inspire us to see our lives as worth living. They do so by restoring our faith in the wellsprings of human value: romantic love, individual autonomy, nonconformity, and the search for self-improvement" (Shaw 2017: 115). In his unique approach, Cavell founded one of the most influential paradigms (in Thomas Kuhn's sense of the term) for philosophical film criticism. In what follows, I consider myself to be working within Cavell's paradigm and broadening its application to a dramatic sub-genre that he never discussed, what I will call the "Redemptive Lawyer" film.

Figure 7.2

After discussing Cavell's contention that films can address our deepest skepticism about the values that make life worth living, I will propose a reading of what I take to be an archetype of the sub-genre I am proposing: Sidney Lumet's *The Verdict* (1982). It embodies the characteristic themes and tropes of this type of film to near-perfection. It is also a perennially popular type, as I will show by concluding the chapter with a discussion of the recent, critically acclaimed original Amazon Prime television series, *Goliath*.

Cavell's fascination with skepticism can be traced back to his early theoretical treatise *The Claim of Reason* (Cavell 1979b), part of which was drawn from his doctoral dissertation. Its subtitle is *Wittgenstein, Skepticism, Morality and Tragedy*, and the first two themes go hand in hand, in his estimation: "In Wittgenstein's work, as in skepticism, the human disappointment with human knowledge, seems to take over the whole subject" (1979b: 140). This is so significant because Cavell acknowledges in his foreword to the original edition that "I have found the [*Philosophical*] *Investigations* . . . more than any other work of this century, to be paradigmatic of philosophy for me, to be a dominating presence in the history of philosophy for me" (1979b: xix). To understand how he approaches the philosophy of film, we must first get clear on his conception of philosophy.

Cavell states: "skepticism's thesis or conclusion . . . [is] that there is something fundamental to or in our existence that we do not know" (2005a: 133). To Cavell, there is a profound truth to skepticism: "our relation to the world as a whole, or to others in general, is not one of knowing, where knowing construes itself as being certain" (2005a: 45). The quest for certainty, initiated by the father of modern philosophy, René Descartes, has proven to be quixotic; his failure to demonstrate the existence of God meant that he never overcame Cartesian skepticism, and nor did any of his successors. Wittgenstein fully grasped the failure of his predecessors, and sought to recast the task of philosophy in its wake. What puzzled Cavell was "how it is that philosophy has required of itself a flight from the ordinary, one form of which is Cartesian skepticism" (2005a: 134). His diagnosis: "an idea of life as inadequate to the demands of spirit is a way of characterizing the motive of skepticism" (2005a: 44). Skepticism has its place, and can be useful, especially as "a methodological, liberating response to dogmatism . . . [but] . . . in the work I have produced on the subject [it is] the aspect of scandal, of skepticism as stumbling block . . . as interfering with the life of my intellectual conscience—not as loosening or liberating my thinking—that mostly has interested me" (2005a: 133).

Throughout his career, Cavell addressed our skeptical doubts about the external world, other minds, and the various proposed sources of the meaning of life: "It is in modern philosophical skepticism, in Descartes and in Hume, that our relation to the things of the world came to be felt to hang by a thread of sensuous immediacy. The wish to defeat skepticism, or to disparage it, has been close to philosophy's heart ever since" (2005a: 245). However, Cavell's approach to doing so, heavily influenced by Wittgenstein, was unique.

In his view, the way around the stumbling block of skepticism is acknowledgment. Skepticism about the existence of other minds is circumvented by acknowledging the pain of the other. Skepticism about the validity of marriage is addressed, in part, by the acknowledging the independent personhood of the beloved. Skepticism about the meaning of life is answered by acknowledging our own finitude, and recognizing the possibility of meaningful self-expression outside the bounds of convention.

Cavell first related the problem of skepticism to the arts in his readings of Shakespearean tragedies in *Must We Mean What We Say?* (1969) and *The Claim of Reason*, though his primary concern in those works was epistemological skepticism. Summarizing this initial application will help clarify his subsequent interpretations of the romantic comedies of remarriage, and melodramas of the unknown woman. Central to Cavell's account of tragedy is his notion of acknowledgment of the other. As noted above, such acknowledgment is his way out of the epistemological problem of other minds: to acknowledge the pain of the other means we see him or her as fellow persons like ourselves, circumventing the problem without establishing the epistemological certainty of the existence of other minds.

The distinction between tragedy and comedy is drawn brilliantly by Cavell: "And it seems plausible to assume that if tragedy is the working out of the scene of skepticism, then comedy in contrast works out a festive abasement of skepticism, call it an affirmation of existence" (Cavell 2005i: 239). Tragedy is "a response to skepticism . . . an interpretation of what skepticism itself is an interpretation of" (Cavell 1987: 5–6). Lear doubts the love of Cordelia; Othello doubts Desdemona's faithfulness; Hamlet doubts the veracity of the ghost, Ophelia's loyalty, and the meaningfulness of existence; etc. In each case, these doubts lead them to a failure of acknowledgment. This failure is tragic because "the integrity of my (human, finite) existence may depend on the fact and the idea of the other person's existence" (1987: 127–128).

This is most clearly illustrated in *Othello*. His very presence as a Moor among the crafty Venetians inclines him to skepticism. Desdemona deceives her father in order to marry him. He doesn't trust her, yet is so invested in her acknowledgment that the possibility of her unfaithfulness crushes him. Then Iago offers him the "ocular proof" of her infidelity that he demanded. The handkerchief Othello gave her, which Iago claims to have gotten from her boastful lover, resolves his doubt and sets him on a course of action. Like the skeptic revenging himself on the world by failing to believe in it, Othello revenges himself on Desdemona for not being perfect in her acknowledgment of him.

In a sense, then, the human condition is tragic, and the reason we wreak such havoc on one another is because of our dependence on (and incompleteness without) the acknowledgment of the other (1987: 127 . . . his account here reminds me of Sartre's analysis of the pitfalls of "Being-for-Others" in *Being and Nothingness*). According to Cavell, tragedy depicts skepticism, and the resultant failure of acknowledgment "as a form of narcissism." He proposes "a reading of *Othello* as a depiction of the murderous lengths to which narcissism must go to maintain its picture of itself as skepticism" (1987: 143).

Via negativa, then, tragedy emphasizes the importance of overcoming one's narcissism and extending the scope of one's acknowledgment of others as fellow human beings. Skepticism can only be circumvented by abandoning the quest for certainty, an insight that led to Ludwig Wittgenstein's reconceptualization of the role of the philosopher from the *Tractatus* to the *Investigations*.

Wittgenstein helped inspire Cavell: "My writing about film began under the pressures, among others, of recognizing a continuous response to skepticism in Wittgenstein's scenes of excess" (Cavell 1996b: 42). Like Austin, and Heidegger, Wittgenstein was engaged in a therapeutic endeavor to get people over their skeptical doubts. But "Wittgenstein's *Investigations*, alone among these influences, describes its methods as 'like' therapies" (Cavell 2004: 275).

Critics accused him of wanting to cure people from the desire to do philosophy altogether. In reality, Wittgenstein sought:

> to join philosophy's own ancient commitment to therapy—namely to free the human being from the chains of delusion. Wittgenstein calls the chains those of bewitchment and of being held captive by images

(compare Plato's appearances); and the methods he speaks of are such as constructing language games, eliciting criteria for the application of concepts, finding intermediate cases, investigating grammatically related ideas (for example between what the meaning of a word is and what explaining the meaning of a word is). (Ibid.)

Rather than sounding the death knell of philosophy, Wittgenstein's methods were themselves philosophical.

Skepticism makes us restless, robbing us of our confidence, and our desire to strive to be who we are. This leads to "[t]he idea of the human as a burden to itself, tormenting itself, an idea taken up by the Romantics in the generation succeeding Kant's. What I am calling human restlessness is for me a fundamental, motivating idea of Wittgenstein's *Philosophical Investigations*," the goal of which was to set as many skeptical doubts aside as possible (2004: 110).

Both Cavell and Wittgenstein were disappointed in how ineffectively philosophy has addressed this restlessness. Cavell reached this conclusion, in part, "from my reading of Wittgenstein, most particularly his *Philosophical Investigations*, where the human being perpetually attacks its everyday life as intellectually lacking in certainty or fastidiousness or accuracy or immediacy or comprehensiveness and is compelled to search for an order or a system or a language," to extricate them from these difficulties (2004: 111).

When Cavell proposed his genre theories of the comedies of remarriage and the melodramas of unknown women, he extended the scope of his attack on such restlessness by claiming that the former address our skepticism about whether romantic love can last, while the latter reassure us of the ability of an unmarried woman to find her voice and thrive without the acknowledgment and support of a spouse. These genres deal with "The issue of skepticism toward and acknowledgment of the existence of others, the question whether we see their humanity" (Cavell 2005g: 150). The women in his favored genres can be seen as experiencing a state of stifled unfolding, which they must overcome in order to attain self-realization. Watching them do so gives us confidence that it can be done.

In the remarriage comedies, the couples separate because of a lack of trust, which leads to a failure of acknowledgment. "In both skepticism and romance, knowledge, call it consciousness as a whole, must go out in order that a better consciousness may come to light" (Cavell 2005c: 7). Mutual acknowledgment is (re)attained by the end of the comedies, due to a combination of meaningful dialog, suspension of disbelief, and willingness to forgive and forget.

By contrast, the women in the melodramas are unknown because they have been denied acknowledgment by a dominant loved one (a mother, daughter, or lover), who has robbed them of their voice. They find it by either receiving the acknowledgment they deserve (in *Gaslight* and *Now, Voyager*), or re-evaluating the bourgeois values that have thus far governed their life (*Stella Dallas*).

In *Philosophy the Day After Tomorrow*, Cavell contends that a "ready dissatisfaction with finitude" is at the heart of skepticism. He thought of Wittgenstein as "the physician of skepticism" (2005a: 44), because Wittgenstein sought to convince us to embrace our finitude, and give up the quest for certainty. I believe Cavell could equally well describe himself as such a physician, following in Wittgenstein's intellectual footsteps.

Having characterized the key roles that skepticism, acknowledgment, and the power of the movies to restore belief play in Cavell's paradigm, let me turn to a new film genre to extend their application to another context.

The law is one of the most fundamental institutions on which civilization depends. If Thomas Hobbes is right, the law is our only bulwark against chaos, saving us from the war of all against all that is our natural state. But skepticism about the ability of lawyers to secure justice under the law has always been widespread, and continues to erode. Research suggests the public are becoming less confident that their consumer rights will be protected when they use lawyers. Redemptive tales such as The Verdict and Goliath reassure the public that not all lawyers are corrupt, and that some public causes are both worth fighting for and winnable.

The virulence of that skepticism is perfectly captured in a comment by Maureen Rooney (Julie Bavasso) in Sidney Lumet's *The Verdict* (1982): "You know you guys are all the same. You don't care who gets hurt. You're a bunch of whores. You'd do anything for a dollar. You got no loyalty ... no nothing ... you're a bunch of whores."[1] Hollywood periodically addresses this disbelief with inspiring tales of honest lawyers winning their just cases despite the forbidding odds against them. When they do so, they are rehearsing the myth of David and Goliath, and celebrating the fact that the law occasionally enables a little guy with good legal representation to stand up to the powers that be.

To my mind, this myth is most ably told in *The Verdict*, and deftly reincarnated in the recent Amazon Prime miniseries *Goliath* (2016). In so doing, they help to restore our faith in the much-maligned system of justice in this country, by showing men in need of redemption doing the right thing for the right reason, and prevailing against the impressive forces amassed against them. Their triumph is mythical precisely because the odds against them are so great, and their opponents are so powerful.

Frank Galvin (Paul Newman, in the role for which he should have won the Best Actor Oscar) and Billy McBride (Billy Bob Thornton, who did win the Golden Globe) are protagonists cut from the same cloth. Both are hell-raisers who were once partners in prestigious law firms, and whose questionable conduct led to their firings. Both are now alcoholic ambulance chasers on the make, scrabbling for their next buck. They each find a noble cause they can crusade on behalf of, and redeem themselves thereby. Both triumph in the face of great adversity, saving their clients, and themselves.

Galvin's retired ex-partner, Mickey Morrissey (Jack Warden), has a plum case for his old friend. Deborah Anne Kaye is left in a permanently vegetative state by being given the wrong anaesthetic during childbirth. The Catholic hospital where she expired is willing to settle with her sister and brother-in-law. Frank can make a cool $70,000 if he simply accepts the settlement. But this will allow the doctors who committed malpractice to get off scot free, with no admission of guilt. He visits the permanently comatose victim in the hospital, taking Polaroids of her. In a defining moment, he stops considering her as an inert thing, and recognizes her as a fellow person. Settling this case would simply extend the failure to acknowledge Deborah's humanity, and betray the moral outrage that should accompany such needless loss of life. In the end, it is his humanity that redeems Frank Galvin, his inability to deny Deborah the acknowledgment she deserves.

Despite being virtually broke, he refuses the settlement and announces his intention to take the damages suit to trial. His old partner consents to help him, and they take on Ed Concannon (James Mason), and all twenty of the lawyers employed by a prestigious firm. But Frank has an ace in the hole: Dr. Gruber from the hospital is ready to testify that Dr. Towler negligently gave the woman the wrong anesthetic, as she had eaten a big meal one hour before the operation. But then Gruber disappears on a month-long Caribbean vacation. Searching for a last-minute replacement, Frank engages a retired African-American anesthetist who now only testifies in malpractice cases. Needless to say, Galvin's case is on shaky ground.

But now he does some detective work. The only person present in the operating room who would not testify was Maureen Rooney. When he first contacts her, Frank gets nothing from her; given her attitude toward lawyers recorded above, that should be no surprise. But she knows something that she will not disclose, because, as it turns out, she is covering up for someone else.

Meanwhile, Galvin's love life is improving. He hooks up with Laura Fisher (the ravishing Charlotte Rampling), an attractive but mysterious woman new to his regular bar. She is very supportive of his efforts, encouraging him to stay the course and pursue justice in the case. But it is soon disclosed that she was a former employee of Concannon's law firm, and is trying to get her job back by spying on Galvin and conveying the details of the case he is making. The disclosure comes just in time to keep their major discovery under wraps until the trial.

When Dr. Towler takes the stand, he testifies that the admitting document indicated that Deborah Anne Kaye had eaten nine hours before the operation. It was on that basis, he contends, that he administered the anesthetic that killed her. But Galvin has a rebuttal witness. Kaitlin Costello Price (Lindsay Crouse) was the admitting nurse at the time, and she had filled out the form, which originally stated the correct information that Kaye had eaten a full meal only one hour before. The doctor had her alter the document to read *nine* hours before, but due to the irregularity of the request, Price made a Xerox copy of the original and retained it for her records. Her ability to produce it at trial guarantees that Frank has won his case, even when the judge rules the document is inadmissible as evidence. The jury not only finds in his favor, but inquires whether it can make a cash award greater than the already substantial one Frank had requested. In the process, the negligent doctors are banned from ever practicing medicine again.

Frank's triumph is complete. But he does not celebrate. He is shown in the last shot alone in his law office. There is no bottle of alcohol in evidence, and he is dejectedly sipping on a cup of coffee. Laura is calling, over and over again, and he knows it. He refuses to pick up. He longs for her love, but she has betrayed him, and he cannot forgive her. He would like to, but he resists, because he has restored his own self-esteem. He has done so with his closing statement, which is crucial to the process of restoring our faith in the justice system:

> Galvin: You know, so much of the time we're lost. We say, "Please, God, tell us what is right. Tell us what's true. There is no justice. The rich win, the poor are powerless . . ." We become tired of hearing people lie. After a time we become dead. A little dead. We start thinking of ourselves as victims.

(Pause)

> And we become victims.

(Pause)

> And we become weak . . . and doubt ourselves, and doubt our institutions . . . and doubt our beliefs . . . we say for example, "The law is a sham . . . there is no law . . . I was a fool for having believed there was."
>
> But today you are the law. You are the law . . . And not some book and not the lawyers, or the marble statues and the trappings of the court . . . all that they are is symbols. Of our desire to be just . . .
>
> All that they are, in effect, is a prayer . . . a fervent, and a frightened prayer. In my religion we say, "Act as if you had faith, and faith will be given to you." If . . . If we would have faith in justice, we must only believe in ourselves. And act with justice. And I believe that there is justice in our hearts.

At the core of our trust in the US justice system is faith in ourselves. In a jury trial, as Frank points out, the jury *is* the law incarnate. We still believe that twelve average Americans can judge when a crime has been committed, and know when justice is done. Skepticism about lawyers is easily sustained by those who do not practice the profession. But questioning the validity of a jury trial involves questioning ourselves, and our fellow citizens. We are inclined to think better of ourselves.

Like Frank Galvin, Billy McBride is about at the end of his rope. A chain smoker on oxygen, a chronic drunk with an oral disease, a has-been lawyer living in a scuzzy motel off Venice Beach, Billy's future doesn't look too bright. He wins our sympathy for treating a stray dog with kindness, and helping his daughter cope with his overly intense ex-wife (Maria Bello), but he clearly needs some reason for living that will allow him to pull out of this tailspin.

Enter Patty Solis-Papagian (a feisty Nina Ariadna), who wants him to represent the sister of a weapons engineer killed in what has been called a suicide. She suspects foul play in the death of her brother in a massive explosion at sea. McBride files suit on behalf of the sister, and then of the man's son, when the sister is killed suspiciously in a hit-and-run car accident right after the suit is allowed to go forward. The defendant is a major arms manufacturer, represented (in a Hollywood coincidence) by the firm of Cooperman and McBride, which Billy helped found. They are the Goliath that Billy will take on with a slingshot.

His "legal team" is an unlikely trio of women: Patty's a real estate agent with an online law degree, Brittany (Tania Raymonde) is a knockout hooker, and Marva (Julie Brister) is a cleaning lady who has had no previous experience with the law. They take on dozens of top-flight lawyers, and end up going to trial without having done the appropriate discovery. Although you always know David will slay Goliath, the story is told in classic fashion, keeping the issue in doubt until the very end.

Billy and Donald Cooperman (William Hurt, as a man you love to hate) were partners in the firm, until Billy got a murderer (who went on to kill an entire family within a year) off scot free on a technicality. This ruined his reputation with the firm (though he was only doing his job), and broke his spirit. His fall seemed to confirm one of our worst fears about lawyers . . . that they value winning more than the public safety. Eased out by a colleague who never really liked him anyway, and divorced by a wife who is also a partner in the firm, Billy has pretty much bottomed out, until this noble cause falls into his lap. He is willing to risk everything in his redemptive struggle against the odds.

Gina Larson (Sarah Winter), the wife of the deceased, had accepted a settlement from the corporation, based on the premise that her husband committed suicide by igniting the fuel of the weapon he was working on. Neither his sister nor his son Jason can believe he did so. His marriage to Gina was in trouble, and she was having an affair, but he was not generally depressed. A suicide note was found, which seemed to confirm the story. But Billy operates on Jason's belief that his father did not kill himself, and digs deeper.

The corporation evidently has something to hide, and the corporate lawyer makes an offer of $500,000 to make the case go away. But this is unacceptable to both Cooperman and the head of the corporation. It turns out that Larson was working on an illegal WMD when the unstable fuel he was trying to dispose of blew up. The manufacturer cannot disclose this without admitting negligence, so it cannot settle the wrongful death suit without risking exposure. Cooperman's motives are primarily private: he wants to grind his former partner into dust.

The climax of the first season is a confrontation in court between Cooperman and McBride, as the two former partners square off about whether Cooperman counseled his corporate client to conduct the illegal operations at issue. Wendall Corey (Dwight Yokum), the head of Borns Technology, had raised the advice of Counsel defense, suggesting that they may have been testing illegal napalm fuel on Cooperman's recommendation. Cooperman enters the courtroom to the swinging strains of Ray Conniff's *Sentimental Journey*, itching for a fight.

But Billy is too sly for him. Cooperman had been having an affair with one of his junior lawyers, Lucy Kittridge (Olivia Thirlby). When he takes her off the case and ends their affair because she stutters during pre-trial preparation, Kittridge seeks revenge. She connects Cooperman to one Karl Stoltz, who contacted Larson and got him to work on the forbidden project. When McBride asks Cooperman if he wishes to change his testimony that he did not know Stoltz, the former partner has a stroke on the witness stand, which leaves him paralyzed and in the hospital.

Billy is investigating this case with the help of a hooker he once represented, an ally that he soon sleeps with named Brittany Gold. Gold helps blackmail a policeman who arrested McBride illegally to harass him for pressing the suit, by seducing the (married) cop and making a video of their having sex. But Brittany is still turning tricks, and doing heroin, and in order to avoid prosecution she agrees to testify against Billy, disclosing their entrapment of the policeman. Her admission of guilt, and claim that she did it on Billy's behalf, threatens a case it looks like he was about to win.

As usual in such films, the protagonist's summation to the jury is stirring:

> But here is the great thing about the law . . . and I love the law. I wouldn't have gotten into it if I didn't. The great thing about the law is that, at the end of the day, it doesn't really matter what we say or think. It matters what you think. That's the beautiful thing . . . I can't tell you beyond a reasonable doubt what happened on that boat, and neither can they. But I don't have to. I only have to have 51% of your confidence. Is it

more likely than not? Do I wish I could convict this company criminally? Absolutely! Positively! But I can't. You see, these corporations are not people. They don't bleed; they don't cry. It's a company . . . When are we gonna send a message to them, to quit telling us what to think, and what we need to be protected from? You can use your voice to say that they have done something wrong. And if you don't think your vote counts, if you don't think your decision counts, you're wrong. There's an old West African proverb (I'm going to be paraphrasing this) that says if you think you're too small to make an impact, try spending the night in a room with a few mosquitoes.

The jury then retires to deliberate. Once again, as in *The Verdict*, McBride's success in this case turns on his trust in the jury, and their desire to do the right thing. The restoration of our faith in the legal system turns out to depend on our faith in ourselves. We believe that we would do the right thing as jury members, and McBride's summation relies on that belief.

In the interim, we see Cooperman in the hospital, helpless and alone. He pleads with Lucy Kittridge to help end his life. He is paralyzed and powerless, and mortified by his collapse on the witness stand. Lucy passionately refuses, though she tries to comfort her former boss and lover. Cooperman has received his comeuppance, a fate that he justly deserves. The jury deliberates for only one day, and finds that Borns Tech committed fraud with regards to the cause of Ryan Larson's death, awarding the Larson family 162 million dollars. Billy meets with Wendell Corey, who agrees to an immediate 50 million dollar settlement, which includes an admission of guilt. Corey reveals that Larson died trying to dispose of the illegal napalm fuel when a snap inspection was imminent. Billy tapes the admission of guilt, and turns it over to the FBI, which promptly arrests Corey. Then he visits Cooperman, who pleads with Billy to end his misery. But Billy also refuses, protesting that such an act would be against the law. His triumph is complete.

Yet like Frank Galvin, Billy ends up alone, back at his apartment (he has no office). He keeps trying to call Brittany, whom he refused to talk to as he was heading to the courtroom to hear the verdict. The possibility that she committed suicide hangs over his head. But he does not take his victory as soberly as Frank. In the final scene, he is on the beach with his stray dog, getting blind drunk. In a gesture he has made before, he wades into the ocean next to Santa Monica pier with all his clothes on.

So, our skepticism about whether justice can be attained is addressed by showing it actually being achieved. The lawyers who we root for are flawed, humanizing them in our eyes. The stakes couldn't be higher, for themselves and their clients. Both protagonists are seeking justice for families that have been robbed of their beloved members by medical malpractice and corporate malfeasance. Hollywood favors happy endings, where good triumphs over evil and the little guy successfully takes on the giant and triumphs against overwhelming odds. Such endings garner success at the box office as well. What the movies do best, as Stanley Cavell has contended, is respond to our skepticism about the deepest sources of human meaning and value, reaffirming that they are worthwhile. This is magic, indeed.

NOTE

1. For *The Verdict*, see www.dailyscript.com/scripts/the-verdict-script.html (accessed January 16, 2017).

CHAPTER 8

Heidegger, Cavell, and Woody Allen: *Another Woman*

Figure 8.1

*A*nother Woman is one of Woody Allen's most philosophical films. Its protagonist is a female philosophy professor, department chair, and Martin Heidegger scholar, who is facing a midlife crisis that unfolds in explicitly Heideggerean terms. So, it makes sense for me to offer a reading of the film from this perspective, after discussing Heidegger's influence on Stanley Cavell, and identifying the themes they share. My reading will also see *Another Woman* as an example of what Cavell called the melodrama of the unknown woman.

Some of my readers may balk at the notion of my discussing one of the films of Woody Allen, given the widespread attitude that his work has been discredited by his alleged child molestation (and his confirmed cradle robbing in his relationship with Soon-Yi Previn). Not wanting to enter into that controversy, I will simply note that *Another Woman* is both profoundly philosophical and one of the healthiest depictions of a woman coming into her own that I know of in contemporary Hollywood. It is precisely the kind of film that I want to discuss in this book, and I would invite critics to take issue with its content from a feminist perspective, if they can.

Though by no means as central a touchstone for him as Nietzsche, Cavell frequently refers to Heidegger, often in tandem with Wittgenstein, because he thinks that "Emerson's picturing of thinking, or rather finding ourselves, as on a path [functions] in such a way as to anticipate preoccupations at once of Wittgenstein and of Heidegger" (Cavell 1989: 1). Rather than focusing exclusively on *Being and Time*, as so many who reference Heidegger do, Cavell most frequently discusses Heidegger's later treatise *What is Called Thinking*, as well as his influential essay "The Origin of the Work of Art."

Cavell's main reason for talking about Heidegger, as I see it, is that the latter's account of the nature of art blurs the distinction between art (especially poetry) and philosophy, a tendency that Cavell welcomes. As he observes: "what Heidegger calls the work of art (he names this work 'letting truth happen') is not to be found in everything we call works of art, and moreover may be found in things we do not call works of art" (1989: 3). This raises a host of common concerns:

> Heidegger believes that thinkers also do the work of letting truth happen ... something of the kind in my reading of Emerson has raised a string of questions: Does it signify that art and philosophy (and whatever else does this "work") are now the same? So is Heidegger claiming that the fate of philosophy is joined (now? again?) with the fate of art? Is our relation to Heidegger's writing (to be) that of our relation to art? (Ibid.)

His answer to all these questions is (in a qualified sense, in one case) "Yes." Let me explain.

In sounding this theme, Cavell harkens back to the writings of Friedrich Schlegel, and his passionate appeal that "poetry and philosophy should become one," which was crucial to "the idea of romanticism as calling for a new relation, a kind of union or completion of work, between philosophy and literature" (1989: 12). So, what is Heidegger's concept of "letting truth happen," and how can philosophy and literature (and, by extension, the other arts, including film) unite in this romantic enterprise?

Well, first we must ask what all works of art have in common: "We must suppose that for Heidegger the working of exactly these works upon us is a revelation of us, our being human" (1989: 13). In this sense, poetry can be as philosophical as speculative philosophy, and vice versa. For Heidegger, all thinking about the meaning of (human) being is either edifying (i.e. life affirming) or nihilistic (Cavell would say skeptical). In his view, true works of art, in whatever medium or form, provide a perspective on the meaning of being, by highlighting and praising certain aspects of human nature, while downplaying or condemning other aspects.

Let's see how this happens in a comedy of remarriage. At the heart of these comedies is a skepticism about romantic love, especially about its ability to be sustained within a marriage. The remarriage comedies answer that skepticism by inspiring an edifying faith in both marriage and love. They show couples that share a believable romantic intimacy, which is based on the firm foundation of their extensive conversations. The couples have split up for some pretty fundamental reasons, and come together again without all those disharmonious elements having to be perfectly harmonized. Like the best of Shakespeare's sonnets, these comedies inspire an almost (but not quite) unshakable belief in love and marriage, in the face of our deepest doubts. The divorce with which most of the literal remarriage comedies begin is bitter, and a good deal of faith must be restored for the relationship to continue.

Like the comedies of remarriage, the *Phaedrus* and *Symposium* (Plato's dialogs about love) function as hymns of praise that inspire us to believe in love. They are appropriately recognized as among the most poetic of Plato's dialogs, and two of the most philosophically insightful. Plato's approach in the *Symposium* illustrates the overlap perfectly, consisting of six speeches in praise of Eros and one in praise of Socrates as a lover.

Beyond their mutual recognition of the commonalities between art and philosophy, there are three other shared themes that ally Cavell and Heidegger: (1) the importance of language, both everyday and extraordinary; (2) the work of art as disclosing the meaning of being; and (3) the quest for authenticity, and breaking away from the "they-self."

Heidegger and Cavell (along with Wittgenstein and Nietzsche) share a fascination with ordinary language and everyday life. Language is so fundamental because: "[As] Wittgenstein says 'Grammar tells what kind of object anything is' (or more literally 'It is essence that is articulated in grammar') [and as] Heidegger writes 'It is language that tells us about the nature of a thing, provided that we respect language's own nature'" (in "Building, Dwelling, Thinking") (quoted in Cavell 2005j: 248). What a thing is called, and how it is described, has everything to do with what it is, or at least what it is thought to be.

Both Cavell and Heidegger also share a unique sense of the strangeness of the everyday:

Both Heidegger's and [my take on the uncanniness of the ordinary] respond to the fantastic in what human beings will accustom themselves to, call this the surrealism of the habitual—as if to be human is forever to be prey to turning your corner of the human race, hence perhaps all of it, into some new species of the genus of humanity, for the better or for the worse. (2005j: 84)

This uncanny take on the everyday is necessary if one is to carry out philosophy's true function: "the uncanny vision is essential to philosophy—to the extent that philosophy attacks false necessities and false ideas of the necessary" (Cavell 2005g: 148).

Taking quotidian reality seriously, and recognizing our everyday condition as generally inauthentic (in which we are failing to be true to ourselves, and which Cavell considers to be the result of conformity), art should challenge us to become who we are, and (perhaps) give rise to some new species in the genus of humanity. What Heidegger calls "becoming authentic" is the vision at the heart of Emersonian perfectionism as well. Heidegger (and Wittgenstein's) central texts "may be seen to advance claims for a way of life, of a transformation of one's life, demanded by philosophy as such and which is characterizable as perfectionist" (Cavell 2005k: 355–356).

Inauthentic individuals, lost in the impersonal social milieu that Heidegger called the "they-self" (as Marion puts it at one point in the film, "well, they said that I'd be traumatized when I hit 50 . . . and they were right"), care little for anyone, including themselves. They engage in idle talk, and avoid truly self-revealing conversations. They think, feel and act the way others do, and hence fail miserably to become who they are. This failure causes them great anxiety, and is the most common barrier to self-realization.

But we are not condemned to a life of inauthenticity. We all have what Heidegger calls the potentiality-for-being-oneself (*die Möglichkeit, sich selbst zu sein*). It is what Cavell construes as the foundation of Emersonian perfectionism, and what Nietzsche is calling for in his demand to become who we are. There is an unattained but attainable self to strive for, and only by turning away from the herd, and exercising self-reliance, can we hope to attain to it. All three philosophers are champions of nonconformity.

These philosophers also share a mutual recognition of the profound impact of the language that we speak on who we are. Heidegger, Emerson and Cavell all seek (as Heidegger put it) to "transform the people's speech so that now every essential word carries on the struggle and sets up the decision of what is holy or unholy, what great and what small, what brave and what cowardly, what noble and what low, what master and what slave" (*What is Called Thinking*, quoted in Cavell 1989: 14–15). Using language poetically, they are engaged in a process of valuation, showing people, activities and things in a positive or negative light. If their language catches on, it can shape the consciousness of a people. This is how intellectual communities, and literal ones, are born.

As discussed above, the heroines of Cavell's comedies and melodramas are engaged in a common quest to overcome social convention and become who they are, struggling to achieve authenticity. To do so, they must find their own voices, and make their unique sense of the world intelligible, both to themselves and to others: "Heidegger finds authenticity demands departure . . . everyday life is a mimetic expression of [and] exhaustive of the value of, everyday language" (2005j: 64). In Heideggerean terms, striving for authenticity requires Cavell's female protagonists to transcend the language of the everyday, and the impersonal they-self that it expresses.

Cavell reflected on the connection between these three thinkers from the very beginning: "The Heidegger anticipation—specifically, through Nietzsche's love for Emerson, and Heidegger's dominating study of Nietzsche—was broached in my first try at Emerson" (2005j: 80). He saw them all as pursuing perfectionism, each in his own unique fashion. Driving the perfectionist urge, in each case, was a profound dissatisfaction with the self as it had been, and the need (yes, even the necessity) to become more in the future.

For Heidegger, as for Cavell, art works make the world more meaningful, by inspiring belief in values that make life worth living. Quoting from Heidegger's "still formidable" essay, Cavell is impressed "when he speaks of 'letting things encounter us' and claims that 'all art is poetry', recalling . . . that, as we are forever told, *poesis* means making" (Cavell 2004: 267). He praises Heidegger for having the "originality to ask what it is that art makes happen." The answer posed in "The Origin of the Work of Art" is that "Art breaks open an open place . . . the Open brings beings to shine and ring out" (ibid.). Let me provide the detailed commentary Cavell failed to offer on the meaning of these very difficult passages.

Heidegger's essay describes art variously as "shining a light," "opening a clearing," and "letting the World World," locutions that have puzzled commentators for decades (and are only slightly less puzzling in the original German). In his bid to invent a new way of speaking of the meaning of Being, these are examples of Heidegger's self-consciously poetic use of language, designed to enlighten us about the work an art work does, by doing it himself. "Light" here is a metaphor for "meaning." Art works create meaning by showing people, events, and things in either a positive or a negative light, influencing their audiences thereby. The material world is meaningless in itself, a dense thicket of insignificant darkness, metaphorically speaking. As one of Heidegger's favorite poets, Rainer Maria Rilke, put it, the function of the poet is to praise, i.e. to show what he depicts in an honorific light, disclosing life as meaningful.

Art works also open up new possibilities for us, often ones that we hadn't considered: "Heidegger, in his *Being and Time*, regards the things in the world called human beings to be such that what characterizes them (as human, not merely as things) are not universals or predicates, but something we might call (harking back to Aristotle, as Heidegger says we should do) possibilities or potentialities" (2005j: 296). For Heidegger, as for Nietzsche before him, art is one of our most fundamental ways of responding to the threat of nihilism. When he quotes in *What is Called Thinking* from Nietzsche's *Thus Spoke Zarathustra*, it is clear that Heidegger shares his intense concern that "The Wasteland Grows. Woe unto him who harbors wastelands within!" A wasteland is a world without meaning, without life or light, a world where nothing is affirmed, and everything withers on the vine. It is a world where all our possibilities seem cut off. In showing a way of life in a positive light, art works can help respond to the threat of nihilism, by peopling a dull landscape with figures whose lives are intended to be seen as meaningful. As Cavell recognized:

> The point is the achievement . . . of what Emerson calls "the sacred affirmative" ("The Preacher"), the thing Nietzsche calls "the sacred Yes" ("Three Metamorphoses" in Zarathustra), the heart for a new creation. This is not an effort to move beyond tragedy—this has taken care of itself; but to move beyond nihilism, or beyond the curse of the charge of human depravity and its consequent condemnation of us to despair. (Cavell 1992: 133)

The classic films discussed in both of Cavell's most prominent genre theories move us to change our attitude to romance and female independence from skeptical to affirmative.

In response to skeptical doubts to the contrary, remarriage comedies restore our faith in romantic love, and its ability to endure within a marriage. They do so by showing couples who have broken up (for some very good reasons) coming back together again. Their conversations, and comic machinations, make their reconciliations both believable and fun, and in so doing inspire their audiences to believe in two classic myths: that they were made for each other, and that romantic love can last forever and conquer all.

The conclusions of the melodramas are, frequently, more equivocal. But the ending of *Now, Voyager* does not strike me as more regretful, or less authentic, than any of the comedies. Charlotte Vale (Bette Davis) is shown in a consistently positive light throughout the film. Her repression by her mother is believable, and we immediately sympathize with her plight. Her response to therapy is heartening, her transformation is stunningly successful, and her romantic fling with Jerry is embraced as a memory to be cherished. Her decision to co-parent Jerry's daughter is not seen as submissive self-denial, but as a way for her to experience the joys of parenthood without marriage or childbirth, and to help someone who was also emotionally crippled by being deprived of maternal love in childhood.

At the end of the film, when she chooses to reject Jerry's narrow view of her "self-sacrifice," we cheer her resolve, and her clear sense of identity. She has authentically found herself, and articulated her world view forcefully and eloquently. Her strength of character is impressive, and her success in shaping a meaningful life outside of marriage does reinforce an audience's faith that women can do so. She has no regrets, and wouldn't have anything be otherwise.

Cavell's account of how remarriage comedies and the melodramas respond to our doubts about marriage, and about whether single women can fashion a meaningful life outside of marriage, has striking parallels to Heidegger's theory of art. We can see that theory at work in Woody Allen's most philosophically insightful film, *Another Woman*, which has more in common with the melodramas than the comedies.

In her voiceover self-introduction, Marion (Gena Rowlands) describes herself as enjoying "a decent level of fulfillment, both personally and professionally. Beyond that, I would say, I would not choose to dwell." She justifies her unquestioning attitude by citing the old cliché that if something seems to be working, one should leave it alone. Especially striking in a philosopher, her reticence to examine her life, and her dependence on cliché to explain why, are defining characteristics of living in what Heidegger called the "they-self." Part of Woody's point here is that being an intellectual is no guarantee of authenticity.

On leave to compose a book, she rents a separate apartment in the city, because the loud construction going on near her home does not permit her to concentrate. There is a psychotherapist in the apartment next door, and she can hear his counseling sessions through the heating vents of the building. At first, Marion is content to cover the vent with a couple of pillows and shut out the noise. But her curiosity is captured by the desperation of one of the patients, who is (ironically) named Hope. Pregnant and despondent, Hope (Mia Farrow) considers ending her pregnancy, and her own life, and the depth of her feelings touches Marion, and triggers a process of authentic self-examination.

Marion thinks of herself as a loving person, but she is told by her sister-in-law that her brother finds her distant and uncaring, and that he hates her. A dinner party that night, in honor of the publication of her book on Heidegger, is marred by a dramatic scene staged by her husband Ken's first wife, whom he left for Marion. She is obviously still bereft, and blames Marion for stealing Ken (Ian Holm) away. Then Marion runs into an old friend from college named Claire (Sandy Dennis), who accuses her of flirting with her husband and of always having to be the center of attention. Claire reminds her that it has occurred before.

The two didn't just drift apart; Claire withdrew when Marion stole away her beau back in college. Marion's response is to deny that she ever had any romantic interest in the man. Claire admits that "I really believe that you may not have realized what you were doing" (*Another Woman*, 1980).[1] Marion stands accused of evidencing another mark of inauthenticity: self-deception. Her self-image has taken a succession of serious hits.

In one of the most poetic passages of the film, Marion goes home and opens her deceased mother's volume of Rilke. She remembers an essay on "The Panther" that she wrote in high school, where she concluded that what the big cat saw past the bars of its cage was death. Then she refers to her mother's favorite, "The Archaic Torso of Apollo," with its passionate imperative, "You must change your life." Just as Heidegger observed, great poetry calls one to be more authentic.

Marion feels she is in just such a cage, and must do something about it. Laura (Martha Plimpton), Ken's daughter from his first marriage, thinks the world of her stepmother, and they do things together, like going shopping and having dinner. When Marion catches Laura and her boyfriend in bed, Scott has the impression that Marion is "pretty hip," but Laura is anxious about what she will think:

Yeah, she is, she's great. She's . . . She's great. She . . . I dunno, it's just that she's, um . . . She's a little . . . judgmental. You know? She sort of stands above people and evaluates them. I've heard her make remarks about her brother, and . . . I always think that she's gonna judge me that way. I dunno. I just . . . Now I feel really cheap for some reason.

This is another indication that it is time for Marion to come down off her high horse.

She visits her brother Paul (Harris Yulin), and they have a sobering discussion. They are sufficiently estranged that his initial response to her visit is "You must need something." Like her father before her, she has always looked down on him, and he knew it: "I realized . . . that I disappointed you. And worse, I realized that I embarrass you. How I live and who I marry." She urges him to work for his cousin Andrew, as his wife wants him to. He notes that she previously looked down on such jobs, and she admits that "Times change." Then he gets to the heart of his animosity.

Once, he showed her something he had written. She said, "This is overblown. It's too emotional. It's maudlin. Your dreams may be meaningful to you, but to the objective observer they're . . . so embarrassing." He tells her he stopped trying to pursue a meaningful relationship with her at that point, so that she didn't have to be embarrassed anymore. At this painful revelation, she announces that she must leave.

Later, a former student approaches Marion in a restaurant. She just had to tell her former teacher that "You changed my life," noting how Marion was a role model for all the female philosophy students. Finding little consolation in this gesture, she has a second sleepless night in a row, and takes a rare nap in her apartment the next day. She dreams she is discussing Hope with the psychiatrist next door, in terms that could just as easily be applied to herself:

> Psychiatrist: What would you say she was suffering from?
> Marion: Self-deception.
> Psychiatrist: Good. It's a little general.
> Marion: I don't think she can part with the lies.
> Psychiatrist: No? Too bad.
> Marion: Not that she doesn't want to.
> Psychiatrist: It's precisely that she doesn't want to. When she wants to, she will.
> Marion: It's all happening so fast.
> Psychiatrist: I have to hurry. I'm trying to prevent her from killing herself.
> Marion: You don't think she would?
> Psychiatrist: She's already begun.
> Marion: She has?
> Psychiatrist: Oh, not very dramatically. That's not her style. She's doing it slowly and methodically, and has been since she was very young.

Then her father enters for a therapy session, and admits that his life is full of regrets: "Regrets that the woman I shared my life with is not the one I loved the most deeply. Regrets that there is no love between my son and myself. That is my fault. Regrets that perhaps I've been too severe with my daughter, too demanding, that I haven't given her enough feeling. But I was so unhappy myself." As a professor of history, he established a prominent reputation by focusing on his career, and damming off his feelings. Marion has followed in his academic footsteps, with far too similar results.

Then the dream shifts again, and her friend Claire is playing Marion in a devastating scene with Ken, revealing what she really wants to say to him. Claire, as Marion, acknowledges what the latter has refused to in real life: that the passion has gone out of their marriage: "We rarely sleep together any more, and when we do it's by the book. It's the same routine. I know what you're going to do and in what order." Then Claire shifts roles, playing the wife of a former admirer, Larry Lewis (Gene Hackman), whose advances she had rejected. He tells Marion she should read his novel, as one of his characters is based on her.

The dream ends with the startling revelation that Marion's first husband may have committed suicide. Fifteen years after their breakup, he died of a mixture of pills and alcohol that was legally considered accidental suffocation. She was a student in his philosophy class, and that, and their age difference, finally did them in. As Sam (Philip Bosco) puts it, once he had imparted his wisdom to his pupil, the relationship dried up. Marion refuses to view the next scene and wakes herself up.

She is in a foul mood at dinner with friends that evening, and afterwards, she questions Ken: "Why do we have to see people every night anyway? We never spend any time alone. Why are we afraid to be alone together . . . Because we've nothing to say anymore?" Ken's response to her decrying the death of their sex life is half-hearted: "I'm really sorry. If I've done anything wrong, forgive me," which does little to assuage her grief. Lost in the "they-self," and idle talk with others, they never discuss what is really important, or acknowledge the extent to which they have drifted apart. In bed later, she recalls a tender moment in her first marriage, when she gave Sam a theatrical mask for a present, and donned it, inspiring him to kiss her through it.

Looking for an anniversary present for Ken the next morning, Marion goes into an antique shop. There, she runs into the analysand she has been overhearing, who is crying over a reproduction of Gustav Klimt's painting of a pregnant woman (the painting is also named "Hope"). Marion tries to reassure Hope that the painting is optimistic, but all she can see in it is a dark reflection of her desperation. Once, Hope had been an aspiring watercolorist, and she regrets having abandoned it.

Later, they have lunch, and Marion, after having some wine, admits that she hasn't gotten over turning fifty recently. While noting that she had never said it before, Marion admits, "Maybe it would have been nice to have a child." This triggers a flashback to her decision to have an abortion when she was with Sam, very much against his wishes and without consulting him. When she informs him of this after the fact, he accuses her of only caring about her career, and her feelings, while caring little about his own. She questions whether he really wanted to bring a child into a world whose pointlessness he had often highlighted.

When Marion eavesdrops on Hope's next psychiatric session that afternoon, Hope is explaining why she feels depressed:

> I met a really sad woman today. A woman you'd think would have everything, and she doesn't. She has nothing. And it made me feel frightened. Because I feel . . . I feel if I don't stop myself, as the years go by, I'm gonna wind up that way. She can't allow herself to feel. So the result is she's led this . . . cold cerebral life, and . . . and has alienated everyone around her. Well, you know, we've talked about this before, how I . . . how I only. . . only hear and see what I want to. That's exactly what she does. She . . . She's pretended for so long that everything's fine, but you can see clearly how . . . how lost she is.

Their similarity explains Marion's fascination. Like Hope, she ran away from Larry Lewis; as Hope puts it: "I've run away from men who I felt threatened me, because the intensity of their passion just frightens me. I guess you can't keep deep feelings closed out for ever, you know, so . . . I just don't want to look up when I'm her age and find my life is empty."

The session holds further revelations . . . Hope goes on to explain that Marion saw her friend Lydia (Blythe Danner) at the restaurant with Ken . . . in an apparent romantic tryst. Marion breaks down in tears upon being reminded of it, and goes home to confront Ken. Refusing to go out to their anniversary dinner, she acknowledges that she should have expected his infidelity, and that she had chosen to look away: "Actually, if I'd had any perception, I would have been suspicious from the start. Because you and I committed adultery for months when you were married to Kathy." Nonetheless, her attitude to him is surprisingly compassionate: "I feel sorry for you, Ken, because in your way you've been as lonely as I have. Ken: Have we been lonely? Marion: At least I've come to recognize it."

Revealingly, Marion soon feels the need to talk to her brother, whose life has also taken a turn for the better (and more authentic). He shares his caring insights with her, beginning with the observation that it is "Strange. Lynn and I go through hell and we're staying together, you and Ken never fight and you're breaking up." This prompts Marion to declare her intentions: "I really do want a clean start. I wanna do a lot of things differently. And that does mean between us, too. I'd like to spend a lot more time with you and Lynn. I'd like to get to know everyone. If that's OK with you."

Her next conversation is with Ken's daughter Laura, who is not surprised by the pending divorce: "If I can be honest, I always felt there was something between you two that was . . . I don't know. Maybe too comfortable, or . . . that's not the right word. I don't . . . Just something, you know?" When Marion tells her, "Well, I hope that this isn't going to have any bearing on us. I really value your friendship," Laura reassures her stepmother that the feeling is mutual.

The film ends with Marion having returned to her writing, and being truly productive. She takes a break and looks at Larry Lewis' novel, to see how he portrayed her. One particular passage captured her eye, because it read like a reminiscence of a rainy afternoon they spent together:

> I remember thinking how wonderful she was, and how beautiful she looked at that moment. And I wanted to tell her so many things because my feelings were swirling so. And I think she knew everything, and that frightened her. And yet some instinct told me that if I kissed her she would respond. Her kiss was full of desire, and I knew I couldn't share

that feeling with anyone else. And then a wall went up, and just as quickly I was screened out. But it was too late, because I now knew that she was capable of intense passion if she would one day just allow herself to feel.

She concludes, in one of the optimistic endings in the history of existentialist film: "I closed the book, and felt a strange mixture of wistfulness and hope. And I wondered if a memory is something you have or something you've lost. For the first time in a long time, I felt at peace."

Another Woman fits Cavell's account of the melodrama of the unknown woman like a glove. Marion never developed her own caring voice, because her academic father was too distant and demanding. Overhearing the analysis of another woman, who desperately struggles with some of the same demons she did, woke her up, prompting her to find her own unique voice, and become who she was. As the psychiatrist said of Hope in her dream, "When she wants to, she will." After recognizing how unhappy she believes her father to be, and why, she knows she must do something. She does not want to face old age as full of regrets as he seems to her to be.

Her conversation with Hope at lunch was both caring and revealing. Her discovery of Ken and Lydia together served to confirm what she had long known: the passion had gone out of their marriage. She immediately decides she must make a clean break from Ken. She then reaches out to her brother, and initiates a newly caring relationship with him. Finally, she touches base with Laura, expressing her wish that their friendship would continue despite the divorce. She has made real progress in becoming who she is authentically, in surprisingly little time.

Fulfilling what I believe should be a necessary condition for this type of melodrama, Marion ends up alone and unmarried. The hope she feels is not in rekindling her romance with Larry. He is apparently married now, and I can't help but think that Marion would be hesitant to engage in yet another adulterous relationship. No, I believe her hopes are grounded in Larry's acknowledgment of her capacity for passion, and her own fledgling attempts to allow herself to feel.

Cavell contends that, in this type of melodrama, "marriage as a route to creation, to a new or an original integrity, is transcended ... a woman achieves existence or establishes her right to existence, in the form of a metamorphosis ... apart from or beyond satisfaction by marriage" (Cavell 1996b: 6). By the end of the film, Marion has fundamentally changed her life, and found a way out of her cage, by striking out on her own. In Heideggerean terms, she has attained a substantial degree of authenticity, becoming who she is to a much greater extent than ever before. Hence, she feels at peace, free from the anxiety of living a lie. The power of such stories lies in their raising the possibility of authenticity, and showing the positive effects that can result from achieving it.

NOTE

1. See www.springfieldspringfield.co.uk/movie_script.php?movie=another-woman (accessed February 19, 2019) for quotations from *Another Woman*.

CHAPTER 9

Halls of Montezuma and the Utility of War

Figure 9.1

War is an ugly thing, but not the ugliest of things. The decayed and degraded state of moral and patriotic feeling which thinks that nothing is worth war is much worse. The person who has nothing for which he is willing to fight, nothing which is more important than his own personal safety, is a miserable creature and has no chance of being free unless made and kept so by the exertions of better men than himself. (Mill 1862: 31)

John Stuart Mill is perhaps a surprising figure for Stanley Cavell to devote a chapter to in *Cities of Words*. But he does so primarily to draw upon Mill's essay on "The Subjection of Women," in connection with his reading of *Gaslight*. In what follows, I will focus my attention on his remarks concerning Mill's general utilitarian philosophy, and on their shared dedication to self-realization, before proposing a reading of the World War II film *Halls of Montezuma*, which explicitly justifies the mortal sacrifices of a Marine platoon in utilitarian terms.

Cavell discussed Mill as early as *The Claim of Reason* (1979b). There, he talks about the changeability of convention:

> it is internal to a convention that it be open to change . . . in the convening of those subject to it, in whose behavior it lives. So, it is a first order in the business of political tyranny to deny the freedom to convene. What that prevents is not merely, as (say) Mill urges, the free exchange of truths with partial truths and with falsehoods, from the fire of which truth arises . . . It prevents the arising of the issue for which convening is necessary, viz., . . . to learn our position on what we take to be necessaries, to see in what service they are necessary. (Cavell 1979b: 40–41)

In utilitarian terms, a convention of the people is necessary to form a consensus on the ends to be pursued and the means to realize them.

Even earlier, in an essay on Kierkegaard (Cavell 1996d), Cavell elicits Mill's authority to confirm his belief that claims about miracles have no evidentiary value. In 1972,[1] he notes with approval that "John Stuart Mill, three years younger than Emerson, says in his autobiography that a Romantic poem had helped him recover from the critical depression that preceded his maturity," though he goes on to express regret that Mill opted for Bentham's vision rather than, say, Coleridge's (Cavell 1996f: 267).

In *Pursuits of Happiness: The Hollywood Comedy of Remarriage* (1981), Cavell noted Mill's contention that a tyranny of the majority is the greatest danger in a democracy:

> a tyranny of the mind—another emulation, now of one's neighbor—[he] looked upon the aristocrat's capacity for independence of thought, a capacity if need be for eccentricity, as a precious virtue, an aristocratic virtue by which the success of the democratic virtues is to be assessed, to determine whether in its search for individual equality democracy will abandon the task of creating the genuine individual. (Cavell 1981: 155)

Cavell shares Mill's concern that democratic egalitarianism might stamp out individuality and nonconformity.

In *Contesting Tears: The Hollywood Melodrama of the Unknown Woman* (1996b), Cavell again allies himself with Mill: "The entitlement to idiosyncrasy is the way John Stuart Mill, in *On Liberty*, describes the form in which, in an imperfect democracy, protection of idiosyncrasy, the heart for it, becomes as important for democracy as liberty itself" (Cavell 1996b: 129). He does so to celebrate Charlotte's response to the question of why she always wears camellias with her evening dress: "Just a personal idiosyncrasy. We're all entitled to them" (1996b: 128). This is a telling sign that she is becoming who she really is, as an independent woman. Mill was a periodic touchstone in Cavell's writings, and he always saw Mill as a fellow perfectionist.

But, in *Cities of Words* (2004), most of Cavell's references to Mill carefully distinguish Emersonian perfectionism from Mill's calculating the good of a potential action, and Kant's focus on what is right, as defined by the intention to do one's duty:

> A favored way of approaching the field of moral theory is to contrast two major theories: one of them, called deontological, takes the notion of right as fundamental ... emphasizing the assessment of human action by its responsiveness to obligation and the motive of duty; the other of them, called teleological ... emphasizing the assessment of human action by its responsiveness to the call to maximize pleasure or happiness ... (Cavell 2004: Introduction)

As discussed previously, the moral dilemmas that the estranged couples in the remarriage comedies struggle with are, by contrast, "formulated less well by questions concerning what they ought to do, what would be best or right for them to do, than by the question of how they should live their lives, what kind of persons they aspire to be" (ibid.). Cavell contends that the Emersonian/Nietzschean imperative to become who you are should take its place alongside the Categorical Imperative and the Principle of Utility as co-equal moral concerns.

Cavell respects the other two sets of moral concerns; it is just that they focus on totally different issues. He goes on to explain: "Teleological theories give priority and independent definition and weight to desires or happiness, and regard a rational society as one which attempts to maximize the amount of good in it" (2004: 67). He is impressed with "Mill's insistence that the principle of utility is both to be the basis of one's personal morality—it is a "theory of life" that assesses my entire mode of existence—and to preside over social criticism, to assess the validity (the justice) of social institutions" (2004: 68).

To clarify for those who are unfamiliar with Mill's moral philosophy, he believed that making sound moral judgment requires one to weigh the potential costs and benefits of all one's options, trying to anticipate their impact on all persons affected. He argued we should feel obliged to do the action that promises to generate the most pleasure (in terms of gratified human desires) with the least resultant pain. Mill called it a "hedonic calculus," which he believed put moral choice on a rational and objective footing. Teleologists like Mill focus on the actual consequences of one's actions, not on the good intentions that people often put great effort into, only to see them go astray.

Utilitarianism has come in for much unjustified criticism. Cavell lucidly rehearses Mill's responses to his critics:

> To the objection that pleasure is an inferior form of happiness, Mill's answer is that this merely shows an inferior ability to imagine causes and kinds of pleasure. To the objection that pleasure is often unattainable or unsure in society, Mill's answer is that this is a criticism not of pleasure but of society's insufficiency in making it achievable. To the objection that pleasure is easy to do without, Mill's answer is that it is indeed commonly, by most people, done without—is this a state we ought to work to make even more common? (2004: 68–69)

At the heart of Mill's project of social reform, according to Cavell, was his contention: "Define pleasure and pain any way you like, society provides too little of the one and too much of the other" (2004: 69). Cavell admits that Mill has his problems (such as distinguishing what is desirable from that which is actually desired), but considers them surmountable. What he doesn't convincingly address is the so-called scapegoat objection to utilitarianism, that it can justify harming innocent persons to serve the interests of the majority (but then, none of Mill's defenders have been able to do so either).

Cavell gratefully acknowledged Mill as a champion of privacy and freedom of speech, in stirring passages that describe such freedom as leading to "the free exchange of truth with partial truth and with falsehoods, from the fire of which the truth arises" (2005c: 40–41). But Cavell noted, with some disappointment, that Mill spoke in his autobiography of how "a romantic poem had helped him recover from the critical depression that preceded his maturity," but once he was recovered, it was Bentham's vision, not Coleridge's, that claimed his devotion (Cavell 1996f: 267).

This is by way of distinguishing what Emerson is up to from the calculation of overall utility that Mill focused on, but, as Cavell puts it, "I am glad to introduce him into our company in working out the relation of perfectionism to its more famous or more respectable neighbors" (1996f: 68). As it turns out, Mill was something of a perfectionist himself. To demonstrate this, Cavell quotes from the introduction to *Utilitarianism*: "I regard utility as the ultimate appeal on ethical questions; but it must be utility in the largest sense, grounded on the permanent interests of man as a progressive being" (1996f: 74–75). What is most utile is, in part, what is most progressive. But what is most progressive will always be a bone of contention.

We are nearing the essence of Mill's philosophy, as Cavell understands it:

> Mill's writing, his philosophical mission as I put it, is to awaken us to the question he poses: Is this, is our experience of the currency of our world, desired by me? It is a question meant to show us that we have a right to our own desires, to have them recognized as touchstones for social criticism and reform. A right, one could say, to invoke the principle of utility "in the broadest sense," (1996f: 79)

Maximizing utility requires maximizing the opportunities to be who you are: "Mill says that a person's own character, his or her own individuality, is one of the principal ingredients of human happiness, even the chief ingredient of individual and social progress. This conceives of liberty as the exercise of individuality" (1996f: 76).

He then turns to Chapter 3 of *On Liberty*, where Mill explains why there is so much unhappiness in civilized societies by bemoaning the fact that people often seem incapable of being who they are:

> I do not mean that they choose what is customary in preference to what suits their own inclination. It does not occur to them to have any inclination except for what is customary. Thus the mind itself is bowed to the yoke: even in what people do for pleasure, conformity is the first thing thought of; they like in crowds; they exercise choice only among things commonly done. (1996f: 78–79)

Here we have Mill embracing one of Emerson's necessary conditions for making progress toward our true self: aversion to conformity.

If conformity cannot be overcome, and we cannot make our unique selves intelligible "[t]hen there is no hope of achieving a moral, an examined, existence together. This condition, which we heard Mill articulate, among other ways, by saying that 'by dint of not following our nature we have no nature to follow,' is one in which, adapting Emerson's phrase, no soul is becoming, none becoming the one it is" (1996f: 80). So, it turns out that Mill is a fellow perfectionist, in the Emersonian sense of the term. For both, individuality demands that we stand up for the values we hold by expressing our support for them publicly.

The epigraph at the beginning of this chapter is from Mill's essay on the American Civil War, where he argued against British sympathizers with the Southern cause, and for the rights of the slaves (how could the author of "On Liberty" do anything else?). His argument that "The decayed and degraded state of moral and patriotic feeling which thinks that nothing is worth war is much worse" than the ugliness of war itself is offered to justify the North's position, despite the unprecedented carnage. In Mill's eyes (as in Thoreau's), if slavery was not an egregious enough evil to justify war, nothing can.

In times of war, the utilitarian hedonic calculus often looks eminently reasonable. Consider President Harry Truman's decision to drop atomic bombs on Hiroshima and Nagasaki. In the first weeks of his presidency, the Joint Chiefs of Staff put it to him as a clear case of the lesser of two evils: either millions die in the course of invading Japan, or tens of thousands die in the bomb blasts. As we had been firebombing civilian targets in Japan for months, it was only a question of scale. It is here that the (Kantian) scapegoat objection can be raised: the tens of thousands of innocent civilians killed in the blasts were used merely as a means to secure peace, and to save more lives than they took. Without adjudicating this particular controversy, suffice it to say that it is harder to object to the argument that the end justifies the means when the stakes are as high as they were during World War II.

Despite this, and rightly so, skepticism about the value of war remains widespread. Given the immense suffering that wars impose on great masses of people, and our suspicion that war brutalizes the men who wage it, it is only appropriate to turn a critical eye on attempts to justify going to war, and continuing such conflicts. The notion that brutal acts of violence and noble self-sacrifice can both be justified in utilitarian terms is common in Hollywood war movies (think of the trope of the guy who throws himself on a grenade to save several of his buddies). So common, in fact, that in *Saving Private Ryan*, the soldiers tasked with finding Ryan and bringing him home to his grieving parents can't make sense of their assignment:

> Reiben: You wanna explain the math of this to me? I mean where's the sense in risking the lives of the eight of us to save one guy?
> Miller: Anybody wanna answer that?
> Wade: Reiben, think about the poor bastard's mother.
> Reiben: Hey doc, I've got a mother alright? I mean, you've got a mother, Sarge has got a mother, I mean shit, I bet even the captain has got a mother. Well maybe not the captain, but the rest of us got mothers.
> Upham: It's not to reason why, it's but to do and die.
> Mellish: What the fuck's that supposed to mean, Corporal? Huh? We're all supposed to die? Is that it?

> Miller: Upham's talking about our duties as soldiers. We all have orders we have to follow and that supersedes everything, including your mothers.[2]

Later, Tom Hanks' sympathetic Captain Miller also has trouble with this failure to add up:

> You see, when . . . you end up killing one of your men, you tell yourself it happened so you could save the lives of two or three or 10 others. Maybe a hundred others. Do you know how many men I've lost under my command? . . . 94. But that means I've saved the lives of 10 times that many, doesn't it? Maybe even 20, right? And that's how simple it is. That's how you . . . That's how you rationalize making the choice between the mission and the men. Except this time, this mission is a man. This Ryan better be worth it. He'd better go home and cure some disease or invent a longer-lasting light bulb . . .

The potential cost of saving Ryan simply does not compute, in traditional utilitarian terms, and the squad assigned to bring him back predictably loses more men than it saves.

In times of war, there is a natural tendency to make films that justify the struggle the country is presently fighting. But, given the horrors of war, it is not surprising that there are a lot of anti-war films (especially since the Vietnam era). *Halls of Montezuma* (1951) was made during the Korean War, by famed anti-war director Lewis Milestone. Most notably, Milestone also directed the original version of *All Quiet on the Western Front* (1930), and *A Walk in the Sun* (1945), two of the most convincing anti-war films ever made. He would go on to make the Korean War classic *Pork Chop Hill* (1959), which depicted conflict as absurdly ludicrous. But *Halls of Montezuma* convincingly justifies the sacrifices made in the fight against the Japanese, albeit in a fairer and more even-handed fashion than the propaganda vehicles made during World War II.

Instead of the indefatigable John Wayne, *Halls of Montezuma*[3] features the far more vulnerable Richard Widmark as Lieutenant Anderson, the commanding officer of a Marine platoon on Okinawa. Their mission is to seize as many Japanese prisoners as possible, especially officers. They need to find out where a secret base is on the island, which has been pounding them daily with missiles. They must locate and destroy it, or too many marines will lose their lives in the forthcoming big push to conquer the island.

The film wastes little time in establishing Anderson as sensitive and self-sacrificing. In a flashback, we see him as a high school chemistry professor bringing a stuttering student out of his shell, enabling the young man to give a stirring valedictory address by the end of the school year. Coincidentally, Conroy (Richard Hylton) is in Anderson's platoon, and struggling with the jitters after the last battle (presumably at Iwo Jima). Anderson reminds Conroy of how he overcame his fears back in high school, and expresses confidence that he will be able to do so again. Reassured, Conroy willingly joins in on the effort, and he and his platoon look longingly back at their original ship as their little landing craft heads for the island (with strains of "Don't Sit Under the Apple Tree with Anyone Else but Me" playing softly in the background).

On the way into shore, we learn (in a flashback from Karl Malden's Doc) that Anderson suffers from "psychological migraine," which, we are told, results from being scared too often in situations where one cannot run away. Doc supplies him with the pain pills he needs to cope with it, while arguing that Anderson has a free ticket home, and that he should think of his future as a teacher. Anderson responds that he cannot imagine going back to teaching after this, and notes that he has lost thirty-seven of the forty-four men originally in his platoon. He protests that he can't run out on the young replacements, or on the seven survivors that have been with him since the beginning.

Anderson is also remarkably humble. When Coffman (Robert Wagner) brings the commanding officer a book as an offering of thanks for pulling him out of the ocean at Tarawa, the lieutenant takes no credit for having done so. Though clearly in severe pain, Anderson knows that he will never overcome his migraines if he continues to take the pain pills, so he refuses Doc's offer on the way into shore. He is, all in all, a thoroughly sympathetic leader, with whom we are led to identify. When Coffman is killed in the first missile attacks, Anderson's migraine gets worse, requiring Doc's painkillers.

The seven survivors from his original platoon are all individuated (we have already encountered three of them), and in some cases are granted their own flashback. Pretty Boy (Skip Homeier) is a farm boy with a dead mother, an alcoholic father and a sister who has just married a Jap in Hawaii. He is a racist punk, with a German luger that he obsessively twirls, who fantasizes about having his own gang. His buddy Lane (Jack Palance) is a soft-spoken ex-fighter who once hurt someone badly in the ring.

At the Command Post for the company, Lieutenant Colonel Gilfillan (Richard Boone) tells his subordinates that Allied batteries have been shelling the reverse slope, where they think the missiles are coming from, to no effect. This is when he sends Anderson's platoon on the search for prisoners, decrying the fact that his men have thus far killed most of the Nips they have captured. Anderson protests that you can't teach these men to kill and then teach them not to kill, and Gilfillan responds "We can teach them to follow orders." When combat correspondent Dickerman (Jack Webb) offers military advice about rocket trajectories and the reverse slope, the commanding officer tells him to stick to his correspondence.

They do have one prisoner already, who agrees to take them to a cave where he claims several of his compatriots are ready to give themselves up. One of

Gilfillan's subordinates thinks it is a trap, while another offers the utilitarian observation that "maybe we invest six men. Maybe we save six hundred." Anderson is asked to take out a small patrol. He responds by also invoking the hedonic calculus: "It's the same old question: gambling the lives of a few against the lives of the many."

Anderson takes along his most experienced veterans, Sergeant Johnson (Reginald Gardiner, in full British accent), who can speak Japanese, and the correspondent. Three of the Japanese come willingly out of the cave, but one of their officers takes up an automatic weapon, cuts them down, and shoots Sergeant Zelenko (Neville Brand), blinding him. They wound the officer, and the rest seem ready to surrender. But two of them commit suicide before doing so, and the patrol comes away with three enlisted men and one officer.

They immediately start to question the prisoners, two of whom seem forthcoming. Romeo (Frank Kumagai) was a guide for English-speaking tourists, and an obvious hustler. He reveals that he drove trucks up the mountain with concrete and rails, indicating that a railroad was being built on which to move the rockets. But neither of the talkative ones knows where the missile base is located. The injured officer and the other man, however, have nothing to say.

Overcoming his jitters, Conroy is point man when the patrol fords a river on the way back from the cave. Pretty Boy engages in hand-to-hand combat with a Japanese sniper, survives, but returns to the patrol hell bent on killing all of the prisoners. His friend Lane holds a rifle on him, Pretty Boy grabs it, it goes off, and Pretty Boy is killed. Lane blames himself for murder, but he did the right thing: Pretty Boy blew his top, and acted against orders, endangering the mission.

Doc is the next man to be shot, and, as they carry him back on a stretcher, he asks Dickerman about Anderson, saying "He's the best . . . Men like Anderson gotta live, and go home. Tell them what it's like." He has written something for Anderson to read, and asks the journalist to clean it up for him before giving it to the lieutenant. He dies as he reaches Anderson's side.

The grim realities of war are brought home by Sergeant Zelensky: "Someone get the dead men's personal effects. Someone get a compass reading of this place. We will have to notify the grave diggers. Someone take their weapons and ammo." Each death of members of the patrol is deeply felt, because we have gotten to know them all. Doc's demise hits Anderson particularly hard, but he soldiers on. They return to the Command Post, ninety minutes before the big offensive to take the high ground is scheduled to begin.

The wounded officer, who speaks English, refuses to cooperate. The sergeant tells him "You must put your mind on different thoughts. When the war is over, you can go back and rebuild your country. You have much to live for." The officer identifies one of the major differences between the two warring cultures: "You seem to have forgotten but, for generations, our people have thought, not of living well, but of dying well. Have you not studied our philosophy? Our Military Science? Our Judo wrestling? Do you not remember that we always take the obvious and we reverse it. So, reverse the role of life. To us, it is death that is desirable." When another near miss from a rocket distracts Johnson, the Japanese officer acts on his belief and commits Hara-Kiri.

Their interaction is especially significant. The message is that the war with Japan was not just about retaliation for aggression against us; it was a war of ideas, of ideology. Japanese soldiers were prepared to die for their Emperor, whom they obeyed unquestioningly, and many of them killed themselves rather than fall into American hands. America was a land of freedom and individualism, where men were unwilling to die without good reason. This is why the question of whether the deaths of so many of the men who went on the mission were worth it even arises in the first place.

Going through Pretty Boy's effects to weed out anything embarrassing before sending them on to his family, the journalist finds an overlay for the Japanese maps that indicates the whereabouts of the missiles. But they don't know where on the map the little square should be placed. Conroy gets killed next, and dies covered in mud, quoting the theme of his valedictory address. "Hope is the mother of all men" are his last words.

The hopes of the company depend on finding out the general area in which the missile base is located. They improve when the third prisoner, who is dressed as an enlisted man, is addressed by an Okinawan farmer they captured by a different name. Nomura/Matsumoto (Philip Ahn) admits he is a major with an engineering degree, but refuses to share any other information. Redemption comes from the farmer, who identifies a plantation on which he worked where the rockets are hidden underground. Knowing generally where the ranch is, the overlay should pinpoint the location of the rockets. But it doesn't, until Johnson applies the reverse psychology of the Japanese and tells them to look for the ranch house on the forward slope. Sure enough, they find a match for the overlay, just minutes before H-Hour, offering a chance that the rockets can be obliterated in time.

On the way to the take-off point, Anderson learns of Conroy's death. Given his emotional investment in the young man, he almost cannot take it, and is stricken with a migraine that is so bad it makes him vomit. We get the sense that the man is at the end of his rope: "Yeah, I told Doc I believed in nothing but seven guys. Now one's blind and four are dead. The rest of us are going to get it too. The Japs have got the right idea. Kill yourself." Dickerman chooses that precise moment to show him what the Doc had written. Though Anderson doesn't want to hear it, the journalist insists on reading Doc's message to the whole platoon.

Doc tells them that if they survive, it is God's will, and that it must be for some further purpose that they are allowed to do so (in Anderson's case, presumably, to return to teaching high school chemistry). He wants them to pledge that those who come out of the war alive will go home and tell the world that war is too horrible to be fought by human beings. Speaking at a time when our lack of preparedness in Korea had led to our almost being driven off the peninsula, Doc's message is a reminder: "Let us never forget that some of what we went through and our losses came because our country was weak. Now we are part of the world, and the world is part of us." Ultimately, the scope of the obligation to promote the greatest happiness for the greatest number is the whole world.

Doc's note has the desired effect on Anderson. He drops his bottle of pain pills, and crushes it with his rifle. He gets the platoon moving, and the missile attack begins. Lane asks "What good was the patrol? Doc . . . Pretty Boy, what was it for?" As if in answer, two quartets of Corsairs fly over and bomb the rocket site, saving hundreds of lives in the process. The success of the assault on the mountain seems assured, and the last thing we hear from a confident Lieutenant Anderson is "All right men, give 'em hell." The film ends as the battle unfolds, to the iconic strains of the Marine Anthem, "From the Halls of Montezuma."

In utilizing the hedonic calculus, we are often bargaining with the future. We are claiming that present sacrifices must be undergone today to achieve the greater utility that is promised for tomorrow. One of the most challenging implications of Mill's philosophy is that the bargain is only moral if it pans out; only the actual consequences (in the long run, for all concerned) matter. If the mission had failed to locate the site, and the missiles had done their dirty work, the sacrifice of so many lives would not have been worth it.

The message in *Halls of Montezuma* is clear: war can only be seen as moral if it saves more lives than it costs. World War II was clearly moral in those terms. Some of the battles the Allies fought weren't worth the cost (e.g. Arnhem), but waging a victorious struggle with Germany and Japan certainly qualifies as, by any measure, the lesser of two evils, when compared to the prospect of living in a fascist-dominated world.

NOTES

1. This book cites the reprinted edition of *The Senses of Walden* that was published in *The Cavell Reader* (1996f).
2. For *Saving Private Ryan*, see www.springfieldspringfield.co.uk/movie_script.php?movie=saving-private-ryan (accessed June 27, 2017).
3. For quotations from this film, see *Halls of Montezuma* (2001), DVD, 20th Century Fox.

CHAPTER 10

Thoreau, Civil Disobedience, and *Selma*

Figure 10.1

Henry David Thoreau was another major touchstone for, and intellectual precursor of, Stanley Cavell's philosophical project. He discusses Thoreau throughout his œuvre, but most insightfully in his detailed account of *The Senses of Walden* (1996f). This chapter will unpack Cavell's analysis of Thoreau's transcendentalist classic, discuss Thoreau's justification for "The Duty of Civil Disobedience," and show how his theory goes hand in hand with Martin Luther King's actual practice of nonviolent resistance to the government, as depicted in Ava DuVernay's much acclaimed account of the civil rights marches in *Selma*.

According to Cavell, Thoreau was uniquely aware both of the promise of America and of how we may have already squandered it by the mid-nineteenth century: "Any American writer, any American [must attend] . . . to the obsession with freedom, and with building new structures and forming new human beings with new minds to inhabit them; and to the presentiment that this unparalleled opportunity has been lost forever" (Cavell 1992: 8–9). Perfectionist aspirations carry with them a dread of disillusionment. Cavell expands on the point vis-à-vis Thoreau: "The distinction of *Walden*'s writer on this point (shared, I suppose, by the singer of *Leaves of Grass* and by the survivor in *Moby Dick*) lies in the constancy of this mood upon him, his incarnation, one may call it, of this mood at once of absolute hope and yet of absolute defeat, his own and his nation's" (1992: 9).

Much of Thoreau's discontent with America stemmed from its failure to establish indigenous forms of philosophy and literature that were not derivative from the motherland: "The colonists fought a war against England, all right, and they won it . . . but . . . we are not free . . . because we have not departed from the conditions England lives under, either in our literature or in our political and economic lives" (1992: 10). *Walden* was an attempt to do so in both literature and philosophy.

The true spirit of the American revolutionary was exceptional: "From what is he supposed to have declared his independence. From society's beliefs and values, then? In a sense—at least independence from the way society practices those beliefs and values. But that was what America was for; it is that the original colonists had in mind" (1992: 10). The Puritans sought "to perform an experiment, a public demonstration of a truth, to become an example for those from whom they departed, to build, as they said to themselves, a city on a hill" (ibid.). Thoreau believed this nonconformist pioneering spirit had somehow been lost in America by the mid-nineteenth century, and thought of himself as trying to reawaken it.

In *Walden*, Thoreau sought to create a sacred text: "This commits him, from a religious point of view, to the claim that its words are revealed, received, and not merely mused. It commits him, from a literary point of view, to a form that comprehends creation, fall, judgment, and redemption" (1992: 14–15). A sacred text consecrates certain values, and inspires conviction thereby. It is that conviction that Thoreau sees as desperately lacking in his contemporaries.

But Thoreau's project had little to do with organized religion: "Thoreau's prose makes it clear that he sees Moral Perfectionism as in competition with religion; it is motivated by a spiritual fervor that makes use of religious concepts, but sees traditional religious uses of these concepts as its most intimate enemy. In this sense, Moral Perfectionism is necessarily a revision or recounting of religion" (Cavell 1979b: 40–41).

The theme of praise is stressed by Thoreau, but in a uniquely American form; his preferred term for it here is "Bragging," which acknowledges its somewhat exaggerated nature. As Cavell puts it:

> But the bragging, while it will not praise dejection or melancholy, will recognize how formidable a force it is, and hence acknowledge and absorb

the Romantic poets' bravery in facing it with their odes. The bragging and the laughter will have to take place over despair, and perhaps will express only that shrill sound. Then it may at least wake his neighbors up to their actual condition. (1979b: 19)

Stressing the primacy of possibility over actuality, this "bragging" inspires belief that America is up to the challenge of creating new meanings to human existence.

Cavell is much impressed by three of Thoreau's most fundamental insights: "First, there is this insistence on what we call something, or what something is said by us to be . . . what is called necessary is commonly a myth . . . our words are our calls or claims upon the objects and contexts of our world. They show how we count phenomena, what counts for us" (1979b: 27). In poetry, or prose, what we call something is all important to how we see it, and whether we believe in it or not.

Second, Thoreau identifies a crisis of conviction in America: we have, somehow, lost our voices and:

[u]ntil we are capable of serious speech again—i.e. are reborn, are men "[speaking] in a waking moment, to men in their waking moments" (XVIII, 6)—our words do not carry our conviction, we cannot fully back them, because either we are careless of our convictions, or think we haven't any, or imagine they are inexpressible. They are merely unutterable. (1979b: 34)

In the period he speaks of in *Walden*, Thoreau had withdrawn from society to seek his voice, a central quest for any authentic individual in Cavell's philosophy. This is "what Thoreau stages himself as attempting to do, as he simultaneously suggests the magnitude of the task, on the opening page of *Walden*: 'I . . . require of every writer, first or last, a simple and sincere account of his own life, and not merely what he has heard of other men's live'" (Cavell 2004: 4). The crisis of conviction that they both describe is more relevant today than ever before.

Finally, in all his seemingly simple descriptions of the natural world, Thoreau pursues the same ends that Cavell seeks: "the writer indicates how his fables of nature should be taken by the human creature. Getting us used to his mythologizing practices, he calls our garments 'our epidermis, or false skin,' which should be changed only as we are changed, not when the world asks us to change them" (2004: 43). Here is another of Cavell's central themes: artists mythologize in order to create conviction, which is best inspired by poetry and braggadocio.

Thoreau uses the term "crowing" to describe this process. Cavell interweaves his own description with quotes from *Walden*: "[The key to life] is to learn not to despair of opportunity unforeseen. That was always the knack of faith. 'Crowing, if it is not followed by the last day, will at any rate express acceptance of that promise.'" Cavell continues in that ebullient vein: "if there is not dawn in him, the crower is at any rate studying 'an infinite expectation of the dawn.' He will then simply glory, if only to reject, to disperse, despair" (1996f: 61). As the cock crows to wake us up, praise awakens us to what is possible. It helps to disperse despair, by addressing our skeptical doubts about the meaning of our lives.

In solitude, we must reeducate ourselves, and "[t]he first step in attending to our education is to observe the strangeness of our lives, our estrangement from ourselves, the lack of necessity in what we profess to be necessary . . . Thoreau's proposal is to brag from just that perch of possibility. If only to wake his neighbors up—" (1996f: 55). Once we recognize that much of what we consider necessary is far from it, the horizon of our possibilities (to use Heidegger's notion) becomes much broader than we ever imagined.

Cavell summarizes his reading thus far: "I have spoken of the sense of loss and of the vision of general despair which *Walden* depicts in its early pages, and of the crowing and trickery of the book as taking place over them or in the face of them. Despair and a sense of loss are not static conditions, but goads to our continuous labor" (1996f: 70). He then explains how we got here (according to Thoreau):

> from our own experience we draw or project our definitions of reality, as the empiricists taught us to do; only the experience we learn from, and know best, is our failure (cf. II, 21), the same old prospects are repeated back to us, by ourselves and by others. We were to be freed from superstition; instead the frozen hopes and fears which attached to rumored dictates of revelation have now attached themselves to the rumored dictates of experience. (1996f: 73)

It seems to be an unavoidable aspect of human nature that we dwell on our failures far more than our successes. This pessimism "may . . . also take the form of what Emerson calls 'silent melancholy' and what Thoreau more famously called 'quiet desperation,' which he claims characterizes the lives of the mass of men" (2004: 48).

But we can temper such pessimism, for "we have not learned in the moral life, as the scientists have in theirs, how to seek and press to the limits of experience; so we draw our limits well short of anything reason requires" (2004: 75). Hence, "Our labors—the ways we labor—are not responses to true need, but hectic efforts to keep ourselves from the knowledge of what is needful, from the promise of freedom, whose tidings we always call glad" (2004: 78). The "moral" of the story told in *Walden* is "If we find out what is foreign and what is native to us, we can find out what there really is to boo-hoo about, and then our quiet wailing will make way for something to crow about" (2004: 77). Cavell captures the essence of what Thoreau is up to in *Walden*: "The quest of this book is for the recovery of the self, as from an illness" (2004: 80).

Conveniently, for my purposes here, Cavell then discusses Thoreau's famous essay on civil disobedience. Like Locke before him, Thoreau thought that political obligation depended on the consent of the governed. But he lamented the result: "That this has made life a little easier for some, in some respects, is a less important consequence than the fact that we now consent to social evil. What was to be a blessing we have made a curse" (2004: 82). To Thoreau, the imperialist invasion of Mexico, and the institution of slavery, had rendered the government undeserving of his consent, and he believed he was obliged to engage in civil disobedience in such a situation.

Thoreau offers a stirring justification for this claim in "On the Duty of Civil Disobedience." He begins by stating his preferences, which sound decidedly Libertarian:

> I heartily accept the motto, "That government is best which governs least"; and I should like to see it acted upon more rapidly and systematically. Carried out, it finally amounts to this, which also I believe—"That government is best which governs not at all"; and when men are prepared for it, that will be the kind of government which they will have. (Thoreau: 39,122–39,131)

It appears that Thoreau was an anarchist at heart, contending that the absence of government is the ideal.

He had several particular reservations about the American government of the time as well. These led him to withhold his taxes, for which he spent a night in jail. It would have been longer, but someone (perhaps an embarrassed relative) insisted on paying them the next day. The experience led him to write the famous essay. His conscientious objections were focused on the Mexican War and on slavery. Of the former, he had this to say:

> The government itself, which is only the mode which the people have chosen to execute their will, is equally liable to be abused and perverted before the people can act through it. Witness the present Mexican war, the work of a comparatively few individuals using the standing government as their tool; for in the outset, the people would not have consented to this measure. (Thoreau: 39,132–39,135)

As is so often the case, the Mexican War did not enjoy popular support. This indicates that the people would not have consented to its declaration, and that it was hence illegitimate. But the general problem is more widespread. Thoreau "associates despair with a corrupted idea of patriotism: 'I sometimes despair of getting anything quite simple and honest done by the help of men'" (1996f: 23).

Thoreau most profoundly objected to the institution of slavery: "How does it become a man to behave toward the American government today? I answer, that he cannot without disgrace be associated with it. I cannot for an instant recognize that political organization as my government which is the slave's government also" (Thoreau: 39,201–39,205). Thoreau summarizes the implication of these two points succinctly:

> In other words, when a sixth of the population of a nation which has undertaken to be the refuge of liberty are slaves, and a whole country is unjustly overrun and conquered by a foreign army, and subjected to military law, I think that it is not too soon for honest men to rebel and revolutionize. What makes this duty the more urgent is that fact that the country so overrun is not our own, but ours is the invading army. (39,213–39,214)

The stakes here couldn't be much higher.

Critics of rebellion and revolution have always argued that one should hesitate to engage in such activities because they threaten the very existence of a nation. Thoreau alludes to Holy Scripture to underscore the seriousness of his recommendations: "But he that would save his life, in such a case, shall lose it. This people must cease to hold slaves, and to make war on Mexico, though it cost them their existence as a people" (39,224–39,226). Indeed, the nation's attempt to achieve the former almost did so, in the Civil War.

Thoreau intended his essay to be a clarion call to his fellow citizens to act on their conscientious objections to their government: "There are thousands who are in opinion opposed to slavery and to the war, who yet in effect do nothing to put an end to them" (39,241–39,243); "There are nine hundred and ninety-nine patrons of virtue to one virtuous man" (39,246); "if it is of such a nature that it requires you to be the agent of injustice to another, then I say, break the law. Let your life be a counter-friction to stop the machine" (39,330–39,331).

Thoreau asks his fellow citizens to join him in doing what he did: "Why do they not dissolve it themselves—the union between themselves and the State—and refuse to pay their quota into its treasury?" (39,298–39,300). He is through with consenting to a society that violates his sense of justice. Most people refuse to engage in civil disobedience, fearing the instability it might give rise to, and the punishments they might face. Thoreau responds to them in a fashion that Martin Luther King echoed in some of his speeches: "As for adopting the ways the State has provided for remedying the evil, I know not of such ways. They take too much time, and a man's life will be gone" (39,333–39,334).

Thoreau passionately appeals to the fellow countrymen who find slavery as repugnant as he does: "those who call themselves Abolitionists should at once effectually withdraw their support, both in person and property, from the government of Massachusetts, and not wait till they constitute a majority of one, before they suffer the right to prevail through them. I think that it is enough if they have God on their side" (39,344–39,346). Unlike Lincoln, who appreciated the irony that both north and south appealed to the same God for His support, Thoreau was unequivocal: slavery clearly violated God's law, and should be made illegal.

Thoreau believed that civil disobedience can be contagious, and could change the world: "Cast your whole vote, not a strip of paper merely, but your whole influence. A minority is powerless while it conforms to the majority; it is not even a minority then; but it is irresistible when it clogs by its whole weight" (39,376–39,380). The disobedience that Thoreau advocates is peaceful: refusing to pay one's taxes is as nonviolent as rebellion can get. He is also hopeful that his appeal will be heard: "But just in proportion as I regard this as not wholly a brute force, but partly a human force, and consider that I have relations to those millions as to so many millions of men, and not of mere brute or inanimate things, I see that appeal is possible, first and instantaneously, from them to the Maker of them, and, second, from them to themselves" (39,530–39,532).[1]

Thoreau concludes that citizens have the right to withdraw their consent to laws they believe to be clearly unjust, and that they should disobey those laws civilly in such cases, in an attempt to change them. Civil disobedience is a right that should be respected in a democracy, which, despite its faults, is the most just form of government yet devised: "The authority of government . . . is still an impure one: to be strictly just, it must have the sanction and consent of the governed . . . The progress from an absolute to a limited monarchy, from a limited monarchy to a democracy, is a progress toward a true respect for the individual" (39,602–39,604). Thoreau's essay has played a crucial role in hallowing the tradition of civil disobedience in this country.

The connection between Thoreau and Martin Luther King's career of nonviolent civil disobedience is direct, and explicitly acknowledged. King read Thoreau in his college days, and, as he put it in his *Autobiography*, "I became convinced that noncooperation with evil is as much a moral obligation as is cooperation with good. No other person has been more eloquent and passionate in getting this idea across than Henry David Thoreau. As a result of his writings and personal witness, we are the heirs of a legacy of creative protest."[2] King became the most convincing and influential advocate for civil disobedience after Thoreau, especially in his "Letter from a Birmingham Jail" (1963).

The film *Selma* depicts a different episode in King's odyssey, the marches he led to protest discriminatory voter registration in Alabama. It opens with Reverend King (David Oyelowo) receiving the Nobel Peace Prize in October of 1964. In his acceptance speech, he declared that "we believe that the illusion of (white) supremacy has destroyed the truths that equality can nourish." Then we are in Alabama, where a black woman (Oprah Winfrey) is seeking to register to vote. She successfully recites the preamble to the Constitution, and identifies the number of county judges in the state. But then the white examiner asks her to name all of them, a clearly impossible task.

The scene shifts to the Oval Office, with King insisting that President Lyndon Johnson (Tom Wilkinson) must act now to change things at the federal level. Johnson wishes to pursue his War on Poverty, and wants to see "this voting thing" shifted to the back burner. He thinks of himself as doing everything that can reasonably be expected of him. King cannot agree:

> It can't wait, Mr. President . . . because there have been thousands of racially motivated murders in the South . . . and you know the astounding fact that not one of these criminals who murder us when and why they want has ever been convicted. Not one conviction because they are protected by white officials chosen by an all-white electorate. And on the rare occasions when they face trial, they are freed by all-white juries. All-white because you can't serve on a jury unless you are registered to vote.[3]

Later, we learn that 50 percent of the population of Selma is African-American, yet less than 2 percent of them are able to vote. But their powerlessness at the ballot box is not necessary, and can be changed.

King begins his campaign by leading a march on the voter registration office in the county courthouse building of Selma. The police rough up some of the demonstrators, and King and the other leaders of the demonstration are arrested and jailed for causing a public obstruction. While incarcerated with his supporters, King talks about the poverty and lack of education his people struggle with, and about a more sinister problem: "What about in our minds? Equality of the black psyche. I mean, look at these men! Beaten and broken down for generations. What happens when a man stands up and says enough is enough? He gets beaten down again."

Meanwhile, their opponent's position is unapologetically articulated by none other than Alabama Governor George Wallace (Tim Roth):

> We will not tolerate a bunch of nigra agitators attempting to cause a disturbance in this State. Not as long as I am governor. Now I stand

here today in the cradle of the Confederacy to remind its people of our Founding Fathers' goals of duty. Goals long since forgotten by progressives and liberals in favor of what they call a changing world. They seek to make us one mongrel unit, instead of allowing each race to flourish from its separate racial station as has been the standard for generations now. Their "changing world" is sickening the balance of the Southland.

Wallace is ready to back up those words with his State police, in an attempt to instill fear in these "outside agitators."

King's case is convincing, since it turns on defending the freedom of his people "to determine their destiny as human beings." He contends that "As long as I am unable to exercise my Constitutional right to vote, I do not have command of my own life." His appeal is unconditional, and stirring: "Those that have gone before us [in death] say 'No More! No More!' That means protest, that means march, that means disturb the peace, that means jail. That means risk, and that is hard. We will not wait any longer. Give us the vote! We are not asking, we're demanding." In order to state this demand most dramatically, King seeks approval for a march from Selma to the State Capitol at Montgomery, which is predictably denied by the powers that be. The leaders of the movement resolve to march anyway, despite the likelihood of arrest and violence being perpetrated against them.

It was their intention to provoke such violence: "We make them do it in the glaring light of day," to appeal to the consciences of the white majority. The goal is "raising white consciousness, and in particular the consciousness of whichever white man happens to be sitting in the Oval Office." Indeed, Johnson's refusal to do anything about voting rights leads directly to the Selma demonstrations.

Violence occurs when the first march is held in King's absence, which lessens media coverage of the event. But it still attracts the attention King seeks: a picture of one of the women demonstrators being assaulted by the police ends up on the cover of the *Washington Post*, much to President Johnson's chagrin. King appeals to religious people throughout the land to join them in protesting these atrocities, which leads to ministers of all faiths massing for the next march on the capitol.

Jimmie Lee Jackson was a Baptist preacher in Marion Alabama who was murdered by state troopers for participating in a peaceful voting rights march, and his death helped inspire the Selma demonstrators. Speaking to them from the altar before the next march, Reverend King stresses his grounds for claiming that civil disobedience was a duty: "Who murdered Jimmie Lee Jackson? . . . Every Negro man or woman who stands by without joining this fight, as their brothers and sisters are humiliated, brutalized and ripped from this earth."

The fight is indeed brutal and dehumanizing, as King's wife Coretta (Carmen Ejogo) recognizes: "What I can't get used to is the death. The constant closeness of death. It becomes like a thick fog to me, I can't see life sometimes because of the fog of death hanging over." He acknowledges the oppressiveness of that "fog" and claims that her love, and the love of their family, allows him to see his way clear through it. But it is an eerie foreshadowing of King's ultimate fate.

King appeals to all right-thinking Americans to join him in Selma:

> While rageful violence continues toward the unarmed people of Selma, while they are assaulted with tear gas and batons like an enemy in war, no citizen of this country can call themselves blameless, for we all bear a responsibility for our fellow man. I am appealing to both men and women of God and good will everywhere, white, black and otherwise. If you believe all are created equal, come to Selma. Join us. Join our march against injustice and inhumanity.

This strikes a chord for liberal Americans throughout the nation, and thousands take part in the second march, which steps off on March 9, 1965.

King is moved by the turnout: "Thousands have gathered here to demonstrate their dignity." His appeal to the conscience of the nation has worked, and he tells them that "We must make a massive demonstration of our moral certainty." There can be no questioning the justice of their actions, or of their foundation in the words of almighty God. When the huge crowd crosses the Pettus bridge on their way out of town, state troopers make way, clearing the path to Montgomery. But white racists line the highway on the other side, and it doesn't feel right to King. Pausing for a prayer, and in search of divine guidance, he trusts his intuition of danger and asks the demonstrators to return to Selma.

But lethal violence occurs anyway. That evening, white racists murder James Reeb, a white Unitarian minister from Boston who has joined the demonstrations. The film contends that the American public's shocked reaction to Reeb's death was what led President Johnson to propose the Federal Voting Rights Act six days later, on March 15. King finally holds a third march on March 21, under the protection of 1,900 members of the Alabama National Guard, and contingents of the FBI and of federal marshals. Twenty-five thousand people enter the state capitol that day in support of voting rights.

As King demonstrated (and Thoreau would agree), the right to vote is one of our most basic rights in a democracy. Black people in America were being denied that right regularly, and their obligation to obey racist voter registration laws was abrogated thereby. Like Thoreau before him, however, King went further. It was the Federal government's obligation to pass a National Voting

Rights Act that banned all the ways the white majority monopolized the right to vote. It was the obligation of every American who believed in the credo that all men are created equal to demonstrate against such discriminatory practices. Civil disobedience, as Thoreau observed, was a way to vote with your actions and not just with a ballot. African-Americans had finally refused to accept the abuses of the majority any longer. The civil rights movement was irresistible when it clogged the racist system with its whole weight, as Thoreau had predicted.

For King, it was not only their right to vote that was at stake; it was their right to life. In September of 1963, four young girls were killed by a bomb in their church in Birmingham, a notorious act that King alludes to in one of his speeches. No one was even charged with, let alone convicted of, that atrocity. The stakes in the fight for voting rights were life or death. King argued that the freedom to vote for the candidate of one's choice was a right worth dying for; in Thoreau's terms, being denied that right was indeed something to boo-hoo over.

So Amy DuVernay's *Selma* is a work of art that both Thoreau and King would have embraced. It is a hymn of praise that valorizes both Martin Luther King Jr. and those who actively participated in the civil rights movement. It is an inspirational tale of a minority exercising its right to civil disobedience, and changing the opinion of the white majority thereby. It is a stirring example of what reexamining the limits of what is thought to be necessary can achieve.

Selma eloquently brags about King's accomplishment, and mythologizes the ideas behind it, in a way that speaks to our time. It assuages our skepticism about whether the corrosive effects of racism can ever be ameliorated, by showing us both how far we have come and what it took to get here. This makes for a truly uplifting cinematic experience.

NOTES

1. Cavell noted the three qualities of civil disobedience according to Thoreau: "Civil Disobedience is an act that accomplishes three things: (1) it forces the state to recognize that you are against it, so that the state, as it were, attempts to withdraw your consent for you; (2) it enters an appeal to the people "first and instantaneously, from them to the Maker of them, and, second, from them to themselves" (CD, 39), because the state has provided, in the given case, no other way of petition (CD, 19); (3) it identifies and educates those who have "voluntarily chosen to be an agent of the government" (CD, 21) (Cavell 1992: 84–85).
2. See www.beliefnet.com/columnists/apagansblog/2011/01/martin-luther-king-gandhi-thoreau-and-america-today.html#Z2loKuojJpjkTCUY.99 (accessed August 15, 2017).
3. For *Selma*, see https://www.springfieldspringfield.co.uk/movie_script.php?movie=selma (accessed February 20, 2019).

CHAPTER 11

Lockean Liberalism and *Mr. Smith Goes to Washington*

Figure 11.1

References to John Locke do not abound in Cavell's corpus. But the doctrine of political consent was a pivotal notion for him. *Cities of Words* recounts how he taught one of his film and philosophy courses at Harvard. Early in that book, he paired Locke with a comedy of remarriage that he took to be an archetype in his original formulation of the sub-genre in *Pursuits of Happiness*, but without reference to Locke. His discussion of *Adam's Rib* in *Cities of Words* is prefaced by a chapter summarizing what Cavell thought to be important about Locke in relation to that beloved battle of the sexes between Spencer Tracy and Katherine Hepburn.

Locke is the father of modern democratic theory because of his contention that legitimate political authority depends upon the consent of the governed. Comedies of remarriage involve estranged couples consenting to reaffirm their marital commitments. Their marriage, and the institution itself, is seen to gain legitimacy thereby, thus addressing our healthy skepticism about whether romantic love can flourish and last within a marriage, and highlighting the need for ongoing consent from both parties.

In this chapter, I will examine what Cavell had to say about Locke, and then apply it to a famous political film that helps restore our faith in the democratic political system (a rare commodity these days). I remember seeing *Mr. Smith Goes to Washington* (my first Capra film) on TV as a teenager, and I identified with the boy ranger who gives him a briefcase from the organization, and with the Senate page who helps Smith, and proudly wears the ranger pin Smith gave him. I teared up during Smith's final speech, and had no trouble believing his colleague's abrupt change of heart and admission of taking part in graft and character assassination (the senator's attempt at suicide strained even my teenage credulity, however). Frank Capra's movies have continued to inspire me ever since then to believe that life is worth living, and that the Good is worth fighting for, and *Mr. Smith* is one of his most stirring creations.

The attack on skepticism that Cavell launched in *The Claim of Reason* had primarily to do with academic skepticism, and the problem of other minds. Locke contributed to the development of such skepticism: "In the unbroken tradition of epistemology since Descartes and Locke . . . the concept of knowledge (of the world) disengages from its connections with matters of information and skills and learning, and becomes fixed to the concept of certainty alone" (Cavell 1996e: 91). Somewhere in the process "the world normally present to us . . . is brought into question and vanishes" (ibid.). As early as 1969, Cavell was relating this brand of skepticism to the tragedy of *King Lear*.

But, in *Cities of Words*, Cavell is more concerned with drawing a connection between Locke's political theory and the comedies of remarriage: both marriage and the founding of governments:

> depend on an original contract or covenant between those who are to be governed and those who are to govern, or, as in marriage, between those who are to govern each other; hence both depend upon a notion of the consent or agreement to the contract. It is here that the idea of the individual voice comes into play. The idea of my consent is evidently pictured as my giving my voice to the contract. (Cavell 2004: 34)

This "original contract" is an aspect of Locke's description of the State of Nature, and of why men found civil societies.

Famously, Locke took issue with Thomas Hobbes' claim that man in his natural state will engage in a "war of all against all." In contrast, Cavell refers to Locke's "fantasm of the state of nature as comparable to a state of peace" (2004: 58). From Cavell's point of view, "The two conceptions of the state of nature fit these two conditions, call them the achievable peacefulness of human nature and the ready bellicosity of human nature" (2004: 61). In short, both Hobbes and Locke have a point.

There are still many insecurities and uncertainties in the generally peaceful state of nature that Locke describes. In particular, there will be occasional rights violations, where there are no standing laws, unbiased judges or systems of enforcement to deal with them (2004: 57). People consent to form societies not out of necessity, as Hobbes contended, but out of choice and preference. Elsewhere, Cavell describes the process: "Consent is always a risk, as democracy is . . . consent is the show of the readiness to change, of allegiance to a state of society responsive to a call for change" (Cavell 2005a: 107).

Like reaffirming a marriage, consenting to a political configuration requires finding one's voice. This is essential to becoming who we are and realizing our unattained and yet attainable self in Cavell's view:

> I take the feature of the voice, or the discovery of my voice and its conversation, as the principal bearing of the texts of Locke and of Milton on the development of moral perfectionism. I think of the bearing as a continuation in our time of Aristotle's perception that it is essential to the idea of a polis, to political association, that its members be those who can speak, speak together, an association, accordingly, made for the human. (2004: 32)

Although Locke proposed the notion of tacit consent (to solve the problem of explaining the obligation of political authority when citizens have not offered explicit consent), Cavell believes that "the contract that establishes the legitimacy of a government, must be express consent . . . what Locke calls tacit consent . . . is insufficient" (2004: 34).[1] As applied to marriage, this would mean that merely staying in the same house together does not legitimate a marriage in any ongoing sense.

Cavell injects his romanticism into his account of Lockean consent. In asking how compromised (i.e. tacit) consent can be made explicit, he attributes conditionality even to the latter: consent is given to American democracy "in the knowledge that its object is still in essential part idea, its existence incomplete. This creates a romance of America" (Cavell 2005a: 108). He calls himself "a booster, refusing uneasiness" about that promise being realized, "and proud of it" (ibid.).

So, what moves Cavell to discuss Locke in this context is the latter's focus on consent as the foundation of political authority, and on participation in the public conversation as part of consent: "It is uncontroversial to concede Locke to be the father or the soul of European and American liberalism, namely of the idea that government is a trust, that it is held legitimately only so far as it sustains the freedom of the individual members of society and is answerable to them" (2004: 36). Locke distanced himself from the utilitarian notion that the best government fulfills the most desires of the people: "Locke's emphasis on consent places him (most clearly since the work of John Rawls articulated the case against utilitarianism, out of a revised contractualist point of view) on the nonutilitarian side of things" (2004: 67). The people must be able to trust the government to protect their inalienable rights, no matter what utility might accrue from violating them.

When that trust is sufficiently betrayed, the contract is nullified, and the obligation to obey the law and submit to political authority is dissolved. But Locke did not take revolution lightly, and his *Second Treatise of Government* offered "a subdued description of the terrible cost of withdrawing consent—as it were of seeking to divorce society" (Cavell 2005h: 159). As the foundation of political legitimacy, trust in the original compact that founds a civil society must be periodically reaffirmed: "Locke's influential pictures seem to imply . . . that each society continuously and in each generation (and in each individual) has to (re) emerge from a state of nature. In lucky societies this reemergence will take the form of reformation rather than a transfer of allegiance to new oppression, or the convulsion of rebellion" (2004: 41). Reformation is made more likely by widespread participation in the civilized political conversation that leads to peaceful change.

A good example of such reformation was the New Deal in the 1930s, where the predominant focus of previous US administrations on the protection of Lockean property rights was modified by concern for the least advantaged members of society (then suffering under the desperate conditions of the Depression). The New Deal was aligned with Thomas Jefferson's contention that one of our three most important natural rights is the right to pursue happiness, as each individual sees fit. The impact of such liberal reforms as Social Security and Unemployment Compensation shifted the consensus of American society on these issues, a radical change that has persisted to this day (witness the recent failures to repeal Obamacare).

Both Locke and Jefferson had their critics, the most vociferous of which thought that their emphasis on ongoing consent made it too easy to justify rebellion against legitimate political authority. Locke's response was uncompromising: "when a government violates or abdicates its trust, *it* is the rebellious party, alluding to the etymology of 'rebellion' as returning to a state of war, a war against its own people" (2004: 46, added emphasis).

In such a case, responsible citizens should seek to reform that government by legal means. Failing that, revolution is justified: "when that [societal] benefit is lost, a given dispensation of such institutions (of a marriage, of an entire government) may be rejected and dissolved—a government violently, that is, by revolution, if necessary" (2004: 34).

Thomas Jefferson made one important change to Locke's specification of our natural rights in his *Second Treatise of Government*. While Locke identified property rights as inalienable, Jefferson thought that the right to pursue happiness as we see fit was more fundamental. Cavell inquired as to the implications of this notion: "Can happiness, or the expression of happiness, be required of citizens? What would public happiness consist in? Is it expressed most purely in patriotic ritual? In viewing such films as are under discussion here?" (2004: 36). In my view, the film I am about to discuss is one of the most joyous depictions of patriotic ritual in the history of Hollywood.

Jefferson Smith (Jimmy Stewart), in Frank Capra's *Mr. Smith Goes to Washington*, is one of the truly inspiring political figures in the history of classical Hollywood. More than any other film I can think of, his successful unmasking of the forces of corruption helps restore our faith in the institutions of democratic government in the United States. Smith was not a revolutionary, but rather a man who fervently believed in the institutions of democratic government, and who worked within them to reform the system.

The leader of a youth group dedicated to upholding American values, Smith is called upon to serve out the term of one of his State's senators, who died while in office. The corrupt governor of the State gets to appoint a replacement, and Governor Hopper (Guy Kibbee) is torn when the party hack he intended to nominate is nixed by an influential group of voters. Assisted by the toss of a coin (that ends up on its edge, leaning against a paper touting Smith's work with the youth group, an example of Capra corn at its worst), he chooses a political novice that his children brought to his attention. He thinks that Smith will follow the dictates of the political machine that runs the State, even as he does.

At the head of that machine is Boss Jim Taylor (Edward Arnold), who has engineered a lucrative public works project that will yield millions in graft. The project is to build a dam that is unneeded, but that will drive real estate prices through the roof for reservoir-front property. He has arranged to have all that property acquired secretly, and his machine will clean up if the dam is built. Taylor ends up approving of Hopper's scheme, agreeing that the "boy ranger" won't know what's going on around him for the two months he will be there to serve out the deceased senator's term.

After getting Smith to agree, Senator Paine (Claude Rains) takes the train back to Washington with him, and they reminisce about Smith's father, a crusading journalist who was shot in the back at his desk while trying to protect the claim of a single miner against a mining syndicate. Ironically, Smith says that the lesson he has drawn from his father's death is that one man alone cannot accomplish much against corrupt political machines, and Paine agrees with him.

When Smith arrives at the train station, he sees the Capital Dome looming in the distance, and irresistibly gets on one of the tourist buses, which takes him around to many of the major buildings and monuments of the city. Most impressive to him is the Lincoln Memorial. One of the most effective passages of the film has a young boy reading the Gettysburg Address for his grandfather while Smith looks on. He stumbles on the word "freedom," his grandfather supplies it for him, and Capra cuts to the face of an African-American man standing there reverently, hat in hand.

When Smith arrives at his office, Saunders (Jean Arthur), his new secretary, berates him for having disappeared for hours. But he is still breathless about his tour: "I don't believe I've been so thrilled in my—oh, and that Lincoln Memorial! Gee! There he is—Mr. Lincoln—looking right at you as you come up the steps—sitting there like he was waiting for someone to come along."[2] Saunders, a hard-bitten and cynical political operative, looks upon his boyish enthusiasm with disdain (at least at first).

For personal profit, Saunders arranges a press conference with the major Washington political correspondents (who all pay her a fee to be included), and he tells them of his pet project: to secure a loan from the Federal government to put a boy's camp on land adjacent to Willett Creek back home. The loan would be paid back by the boys themselves, and Smith is proud to say that it would hence not contribute to the burden of debt that the Federal government is already carrying. It turns out that the dam Taylor is planning to propose to Congress is on the same Creek. This sets up the dramatic confrontation at the heart of this drama.

At first, they try to distract Smith, by having Senator Paine's gorgeous daughter Susan (Astrid Allwyn) arrange to see Mount Vernon with him at the same time as the Senate session in which the bill for the dam is proposed. Saunders sets up the date, but gags on such treachery and later fills him in on the scam. While she helps him frame his bill for the camp, Smith inspires her with his talk about capturing something of the essence of the Capitol Building in the proposal. As he puts it:

> I want to make that [the Capitol Dome] comes to life—yes, and lighted up like that, too—for every boy in the land. Boys forget what their country means—just reading "land of the free" in history books. And they get to be men—and forget even more. Liberty is too precious to get buried in

books, Miss Saunders. Men ought to hold it up in front of them—every day of their lives and say: "I am free—to think—to speak. My ancestors couldn't. I can. My children will."

One gets a sense that Capra may have been speaking in the first person here, but this speech may well have been written by Sidney Buchman (who won the Academy Award for Best Screenplay that year).

Crucial to our belief in this idealist is the transformation that Saunders undergoes because of his inspiring influence. After describing the idyllic setting of his camp to her, he continues:

> Everybody ought to have some of that—sometime in his life. My father taught me to see those things. He grew up with our state—an' he used to say to me, "Son, don't miss the wonders that surround you. Every tree, every sunset, every ant-hill and star is filled with the wonders of nature." He used to say, "Haven't you ever noticed how grateful you are to see daylight again after going through a dark tunnel?" "Well," he'd say, "open your eyes and always see life around you as if you'd just come out of a long tunnel."

When he turns and asks her where she comes from, Saunders responds quietly, "Well—I guess I've been in that tunnel."

Being eaten alive by her newly awakened conscience, she goes out and gets drunk with her old friend Diz (Thomas Mitchell), one of the Washington correspondents. He has asked her to marry him before, and tonight she says she is ready. But all she talks about is Smith, and finally she drags Diz to Smith's office, and spills the beans:

> Want to be a Senator, huh? Gonna build a camp on Willet Creek! See this? Appropriations Bill. A little section—number forty. A dam's going up where you think you're gonna have a camp. Ever hear of it? No. They read all about it in the Senate today—but you weren't supposed to hear it. That's why that ritzy dame took you in tow. That's why they sent you here in the first place—because you wouldn't know a dam from a bathtub! Go ahead—try to build your camp—try to mess up Mr. Taylor's little graft! Go ahead—be a Senator! But if you can't—and you can't in nine million years—go on home—don't hang around here making people feel sorry for you!

She then asks Diz to take her home.

The next morning, Smith heads for the Senate, ready to speak out against the deficiency bill that contains the dam project. But when he is recognized by the Vice President (Harry Carey), he yields to his colleague Senator Paine, who launches a vicious attack on the junior senator, cooked up by the Taylor Machine. Following his own recommendation that, in politics, one has to leave one's ideals outside the door, Paine accuses Smith of having bought up the property around Willett Creek, and of enriching himself by taking advantage of all the little boy rangers, who mailed in their nickels and dimes to pay for the camp. The Senate committee holds a hearing on these charges, and Smith refuses to speak up in his defense, rushing out of the hearing room in a manner that makes him look guilty as sin.

When he doesn't show up at his office by evening, Saunders knows where to find him: at the Lincoln Memorial. Sure enough, he is there, weeping in the depths of his disillusionment. He has apparently given up, and thinks his quest was ridiculous to begin with: "An honorary stooge like me against the Taylors and Paines.—The machines and the lies." But Saunders won't let him do so. Shaming him for his hesitance, she asks him what he'll tell the young boys when he goes back home. She exhorts him to keep trying, in the speech of Jean Arthur's career:

> Your friend Mr. Lincoln had his Taylors and Paines. So has every man who ever tried to lift his thought up off the ground. Odds against them didn't stop them, they were fools that way. All the good in this world came from fools with faith like that. You can't quit now. Not you. They aren't all Taylors and Paines, that kind just throw big shadows. You didn't just have faith in Paine or any other man. It was bigger than that. You had plain, decent, everyday common rightness. The Country could use some of that. So could the whole cock-eyed world. A lot of it. Remember the first day you got here? What you said about Mr. Lincoln? You said he was sitting there waiting for someone. You were right. He was waiting for a man who could see his job and sail into it. A man who could tear into the Taylors and root them out into the open. I think he was waiting for you, Jeff.

Her plan is to use one of the hallowed procedures of the Senate to hold up the deficiency bill. Smith will stage a filibuster.

The significance of this event is underscored by having the most renowned radio newsman of the time report on its occurrence:

> This is H. V. Kaltenborn speaking—half of official Washington is here to see democracy's finest show—Washington's uncontrolled filibuster. The right to talk your head off . . . The American privilege of free speech in its most dramatic form . . . the least man in that chamber, once he gets and holds the floor by the rules, can hold it and talk as long as he can stand on

his feet—providing always first, that he does not sit down, second that he does not leave the chamber or stop talking. The galleries are packed, and in the diplomatic gallery are the envoys of two dictator powers. They have come to see what they can't see at home—democracy in action.

Coached by Saunders, who is up in the Senate gallery, Smith will hold the floor for the next twenty-three hours.

He reads the Constitution, and the Declaration of Independence, trying to explain his cause: "You see, that's what I had in mind about the camp—except those men said it a little better than I can. Now, you're not gonna have a country that makes these kinds of rules work, if you haven't got men who've learned to tell human rights from a punch in the nose." He goes on to explain his plan for bringing children of different nationalities and races together, celebrating their common values as Americans and "finding out what makes different people tick the way they do. 'Cause I wouldn't give you a red cent for all your fine rules, without there being some plain every day, common kindness under 'em—and a little looking-out for the next fella. Yes—pretty important, all that. Just happens to be blood and bone and sinew of this democracy."

Smith's hyper-dramatic summation, his voice failing him after twenty-three hours of continuous speaking, states his commitments most emphatically:

> there just can't be any compromise with inalienable rights like life and liberty. That's about the only thing I know for sure . . . Just get up off the ground, that's all I ask. Get up there with that lady that is up on top of this Capitol Dome—that lady that stands for liberty, take a look at this country through her eyes if you really want to see something and you won't just see scenery—you'll see the whole parade of what man's carved out for himself after centuries of fighting and fighting for something better than just jungle law, fighting so's he can stand on his own two feet—free and decent, like he was created—no matter what his race, color or creed. That's what you'll see. There's no place out there for graft or greed or lies or compromise with human liberties.

He then turns to Paine directly, admits that his is probably a lost cause, and reminds Paine that his father always said those were the only causes worth fighting for. Paine was once an idealist himself, who also championed such lost causes alongside the senior Mr. Smith, but he tells himself (and Smith) that he had compromised those ideals for the sake of the good he could do in his position of power.

Hoping to finish Smith off, Paine brings in thousands of telegrams generated by the Taylor Machine, all calling for Smith to end his filibuster and resign. He protests that he is not licked yet, and then faints dead away on the

Senate floor. This is too much for Paine to take. He goes out into the Senate antechamber and tries to shoot himself in the head. After being saved from carrying out his rash intention by a concerned colleague, Paine reenters the Senate chamber, admits his role in the graft plot, and confirms that everything Smith has been saying is true. Smith comes to, and our Senate page signals Saunders that he is OK. The film ends with the Vice President putting his feet up on his presiding desk and chewing a stick of gum, clearly pleased with how the proceedings had turned out.

Though popular at the box office, it was surprising to me (but not to Capra, who expected controversy) that *Mr. Smith* stirred up a hornets' nest of contemporary critics. Capra was accused of being downright un-American. Senate Majority Leader Barkley protested that "it showed the Senate as the biggest aggregation of nincompoops on record," and democratic Senator Byrnes complained that "here is a picture that is going to the country to tell it that 95 out of 96 Senators are corrupt."

Senator Paine pleaded with Smith to "be reasonable" and give his consent to the deficiency bill. Paine sounds reasonable at first, but reveals his corrupt nature by the time he has finished his plea:

> you've had no experience—you see things as black or white—and a man as angel or devil. That's the young idealist in you. And that isn't how the world runs, Jeff—certainly not Government and politics. It's a question of give and take—you have to play by the rules—compromise—you have to leave your ideals outside the door, with your rubbers. I feel I'm the right man for the Senate. And there are certain powers with influence. To stay there, I must respect them. And now and then—for the sake of that power—a dam has to be built—and one must shut his eyes. It's—it's a small compromise. The best men have had to make them. Do you understand? I know how you feel, Jeff. Thirty years ago—I had those ideals, too. I was you. I had to make the decision you were asked to make today. And I compromised—yes! So that all these years I could stay in that Senate—and serve the people in a thousand honest ways! You've got to face facts, Jeff. I've served our State well, haven't I? We have the lowest unemployment and the highest Federal grants. But, well, I've had to compromise, had to play ball. You can't count on people voting, half the time they don't vote, anyway. That's how states and empires have been built since time began.

At the end, Paine even assaults the notion that the legitimacy of a government depends on the voters. In his mind, if the benefits of colluding in corruption outweigh the costs, he is perfectly justified in playing along with the powers that be.

Smith's response is an unequivocal no. He states his position during his filibuster: "—there just can't be any compromise with inalienable rights like life and liberty. That's about the only thing I know for sure." This clearly hearkens back to John Locke's contention that inalienable individual rights should not be violated to serve the common good. Individuals can only protect their rights if the legitimate power of governments continues to depend upon their ongoing consent. Smith refuses to go along in order to get along, even after Taylor offers him his Senate seat for the foreseeable future if he will look the other way on the dam.

It is no coincidence that Capra's most passionate praise of our democratic institutions was crafted under the looming shadow of World War II. It was a time when Americans desperately needed to be reassured, and *Mr. Smith Goes to Washington* fitted the bill perfectly.

NOTES

1. "While there are of course some general obligations and rights that all people have from the law of nature, special obligations come about only when people voluntarily undertake them. Locke clearly states that one can only become a full member of society by an act of express consent" (*Two Treatises of Government*: 2.122): see *Stanford Encyclopedia of Philosophy*, entry on Locke's Political Philosophy, available at https://plato.stanford.edu/entries/locke-political/ (accessed August 13, 2017).
2. All quotes from the film are taken from www.script-o-rama.com/movie_scripts/m/mr-smith-goes-to-washington-script.html (accessed August 15, 2017).

CHAPTER 12

Cavell's Notion of Acknowledgment and *Boys Don't Cry*

Figure 12.1

The concept of acknowledgment plays a crucial role at several junctures in the corpus of Stanley Cavell, as I have noted. It is so central that it deserves its own chapter, as a coda to this book. In what follows, I will survey his various pronouncements on the subject, and then turn to an analysis of *Boys Don't Cry* that foregrounds the notion. This film, based on a 1990s' real-life tragedy in Nebraska, begins with an episode in which a biologically female adolescent comes to self-identify as male. The film can best be read as a personal odyssey in which he moves to a new location and seeks acknowledgment from others of his transgendered identity.

The Bing search engine defines acknowledgment as "the action of expressing or displaying gratitude or appreciation for something," stating that the term's synonyms include "thanks, praise, acceptance, recognition and respect." This comes pretty close to capturing how Stanley Cavell uses the term. He started doing so as early as 1969, in *Must We Mean What We Say: A Book of Essays*,[1] and he wielded his favorite conceptual tool to address some of the most profound philosophical and artistic issues that interested him.

In those initial essays, Cavell mobilizes the concept to both solve the problem of other minds and account for the essence of the tragedy of *King Lear*. Cartesian skepticism, which led directly to the position of solipsism, can only be successfully addressed by giving up the demand for certainty, which is a challenge: "But how do we stop? How do we learn that what we need is not more knowledge but the willingness to forego knowledge? . . . [we must come to realize that] The world is to be accepted, as the presentness of other minds is not to be known but acknowledged" (Cavell 1996e: 92). When we see, for example, that other persons are in pain, and verbally or gesturally acknowledge it to them, we have the best evidence for other minds that we can hope to find.

Cavell explains how this constitutes a response to skepticism in a later work: "The answer does not consist in denying the conclusion of skepticism but in reconceiving its truth. It is true that we do not know the existence of the world with certainty; our relation to its existence is deeper—one in which it is accepted, that is to say, received. My favorite way of putting this is to say that existence is to be acknowledged" (Cavell 1992: 133).

Turning to the second issue, Cavell contends that *King Lear* is the tragedy of a man who is desperate for love, but skeptical about whether he can be loved. His gambit of determining how he will parcel out his kingdom to his daughters on the basis of who loves him most is the act of a man who doubts whether he is worthy of being loved in his own right. He accepts the flattery of Goneril and Regan, though he knows it rings false. He rejects Cordelia's unadorned expressions of her respect and love for him, which ring true, because of his own monumental insecurity. She acknowledges him, but he withholds his acknowledgment of her, which leads directly to the tragic *denouement*.

Why does he do so? Cavell contends that it is because he has little love to give in return. He fears losing the love of his daughters when he relinquishes power: "Mortality, the hand without rings of power on it, cannot be lovable. He feels unworthy of love when the reality of his lost power comes over him. This is what his plan was to have avoided by exchanging his fortune for his love. He cannot bear love when he has no reason to be loved" (Cavell 1996e: 26). Cordelia succinctly expresses her love for Lear ("Good my lord, you have begot me, bred me, loved me: I return those duties back as are right fit, Obey you, love you, and most honour you"), but not in the form he wants to hear. She will not engage in the exaggerated flattery that her sisters offered, and in refusing to do so, "[s]he threatens to expose his plan to return false love with no love, and expose the necessity for that plan—his terror of being loved, of needing love" (1996e: 27). Cavell concludes that *King Lear* is a tragedy about the avoidance of love.

In both cases, Cavell demonstrates the fruitfulness of the concept of acknowledgment. But he is just getting started. In an essay entitled "Knowing and Acknowledging," he describes the phenomenon of sympathy in stirring terms: "your suffering makes a claim on me. It is not enough that I know that you suffer—I must do or reveal something . . . in a word I must acknowledge it, otherwise I do not know what '(your or his) being in pain' means. Is" (Cavell 1996e: 68). It is attendant upon anyone who sees another person in pain to recognize it: "'A failure to acknowledge' is the expression of something, a confusion, an indifference, a callousness, an exhaustion, a coldness. Spiritual emptiness is not a blank" (1996e: 69). Respect for others obliges us to recognize their suffering.

Cavell accounts for the comedies of remarriage thereby as well: "I discuss the amatory wars of the comedies as struggles for acknowledgment" (Cavell 1996b: 30). Furthermore, "the struggle is for the reciprocity or equality of consciousness, between a woman and a man, a study of the conditions under which this fight for recognition (as Hegel put it) or demand for acknowledgment (as I have put it) is a struggle for mutual freedom" (Cavell 1981: 17, 18). In the comedies, the struggle ends fruitfully, and mutual acknowledgment is attained.

What, exactly, does the sought-after acknowledgment amount to in a romantic relationship? First of all, each member of the couple must acknowledge themselves to be who they are. One or both members of the unhappy couple have failed to do that in the past, and this is a scary prospect. Once having recognized who they are, how should they proceed to try to recognize their spouse? On Cavell's view, true acknowledgment of a person as one's beloved involves two essential elements.

Most importantly, it requires "finding the means of expressing praise, of acknowledging mutuality with another, gratitude for another's existence, as for one's own"(Cavell 2005a: 68). Cavell asks "What is it about praise that it should emerge as an essential topic of the examination of our acknowledgment of the existence of others?" (2005a: 3). His answer is that praise helps us to uncover the true meaning of being, as I discussed in the chapter on Heidegger and *Another Woman*. This connects directly to the definition with which this chapter began. Praise is how we should express our appreciation and gratitude for the existence of the other, and for their love of us. Being true, it helps point the way to their authentic self. Being positive, it inspires confidence in them to strive to be all they can be, the essential project of Emersonian perfectionism.

But praising the beloved is not enough: "How is acknowledgment expressed; that is, how do we put ourselves in another's presence? . . . By revealing ourselves. When we do not, when we keep ourselves in the dark, the consequence is that we convert the other into a character and make the world a stage for him" (2005a: 149). Therefore, "the completion of acknowledgment requires self-revelation" (2005a: 153). To become truly vulnerable to our beloved. we must have the courage to be ourselves, to disclose ourselves to the other as we are. Hence the truism that (like Lear) you cannot love another if you do not love yourself.

One of the major contrasts between the comedies and the melodramas that Cavell discusses is that:

> [I]n the melodramas this struggle [for mutual recognition] is renounced: the man's struggle there is, on the contrary, a struggle against recognition. The woman's struggle is to understand why recognition by the man has not happened or has been denied, or has become irrelevant, hence may be thought of as a struggle or argument (with herself) over her gender. (1996b: 30)

But this is not the only sense in which acknowledgment is relevant to appreciating the melodramas.

The women in the melodramas are unknown precisely because they have been denied acknowledgment as independent selves by their parents (*Now, Voyager* and *The Heiress*), lovers (*Letter from an Unknown Woman, Gaslight*), or children (*Stella Dallas*). As a result, they have been unable to find their own voice and become who they are. Their struggle is to free themselves from the need for recognition from these dominating others, and to discover their sense of autonomous selfhood in its absence.

The heroines in these melodramas attain self-acknowledgment, in some cases with the help of the recognition of their worth from a friend (e.g. Charlotte with the aid of Dr. Jaquith). It is their ability to do so that refutes our skepticism about whether women can find themselves, and lead a fulfilling life, outside of marriage. Cavell's accounts of both genres foreground the importance of recognition from the romantic other, with the comedies depicting its attainment and the melodramas showing us women who have forsaken the search for it.

Boys Don't Cry is neither a comedy nor a melodrama. Teena Brandon (Hilary Swank), so named in accordance with our cultural conventions about human biology, is experimenting with the prospect of identifying as male gendered. It is clear from the film's narrative that the shift to calling herself Brandon Teena is an expression born of genuine conviction. It is possible to read Teena Brandon as a ne'er do well who is on her own, and who simply decides to adopt a masculine persona for kicks while staying with her cousin in his trailer. But I don't interpret him as so ambiguous about his gender identity (and I will use the masculine pronoun hereafter).

Brandon is a real hit with the ladies, coming off as a sensitive guy with a rebellious streak. He also attracts the hostility of a group of young men, who chase him back to the trailer. His cousin Lonny grills him about what happened:

Lonny: What is the matter with you?
Brandon: I don't know! I don't know what went wrong!
Lonny: You are not a boy! That is what went wrong! You are not a boy!
Brandon: They say I'm the best boyfriend they ever had.
Lonny: Do you want your mother to lock you up again? Is that what you want?
Brandon: No.
Lonny: Then why don't you just admit that you're a dyke?
Brandon: Because I'm not a dyke.[2]

So, from the very beginning, he clearly and unequivocally acknowledges that he is transgender, albeit one who cannot afford surgery, or all of the expensive hormones, that enable the biological transition (though he carries the literature about such procedures with him). With regard to bodily gender aesthetics, he must content himself with binding his breasts and padding his crotch.

The cousin has had enough of him, and the trouble he gets into, and throws him out. He goes to a bar, and fatefully meets a young woman named Candace (Alicia Goranson), who takes to him immediately. He goes to get them some cigarettes, and returns to find that a tough-looking guy has taken his place and is hitting on Candace, who rejects these crude advances. Brandon asks the man to back off, and gets punched out for his trouble. Candace's friends John (Peter Sarsgaard) and Tom (Brendan Sexton) intervene, help stop an impending beating, and then ask him if he wants to go to a party with the three of them. Delighted with their apparent acceptance of him, Brandon tags along.

The party is in Falls City, a small town seventy miles south of Lincoln. He has a good time, and asks them if he can stay over. They take him in, to a house owned by an older woman with a drinking problem, and a daughter named Lana (Chloe Sevigny). John is Lana's former boyfriend, and it is unclear how he and his friend came to live with them. They accept Brandon and welcome him into their house, believing him to be a boy.

Brandon takes an immediate liking to Lana, and vice versa. He is exhilarated by his newfound freedom in a little town where no one knows he is transgender, and everyone seems to like him. His infectious smile is attractive, and his willingness to play such masculine games as hanging off the end of a pickup truck by a rope (so-called "bumper skiing") puts him in good stead with the guys. When Lana asks him why he lets them drag him around by a rope like a dog, Brandon tells her "I just thought that's what guys do around here." He is attentively taking lessons in masculinity.

The early scenes in Falls City are electric. Brandon is having the time of his life. His smile lights up the screen, and there is a holiday in his eyes. We get the feeling that his new masculine persona allows him to become who he is, which clearly feels great. Brandon gets to know John a little, who tells him about being in prison, and how Lana wrote him letters when he was inside, and that she and her mom took John into their home when he got out.

Brandon, for his part, makes up stories about his life, telling them that his dad (who is dead) lives in Memphis, his mom is out in Hollywood, and his sister is a model. Lana's mother examines his face closely, telling him she believes he has a sister who's a model, because "You're like a little movie star yourself." The young people all go joyriding, and Brandon takes the wheel when John is too drunk. He is having a blast driving at eighty mph down a country road, until the cops come and pull him over. He gets lucky when they can't check his priors because their computer is down, and gets off with a ticket.

Brandon has to return to Lincoln for a court date, on the charge of stealing a car. He stays with his cousin again, who warns him about Falls City: "They hang faggots down there." He tells the cousin that he is going to ask Lana to marry him, who responds with two reasonable questions: "Before or after your sex-change operation? Before or after you tell her you're a girl?" Brandon reassures him that "it's different. It's workin'. I'm not gonna fuck it up this time," but his cousin responds with continuing concern: "I hope they do lock you up tomorrow."

Brandon shows up in court, but cuts out before his name is called, resulting in a bench warrant being issued for his arrest. He returns to Falls City, and has a sexual encounter with Lana, where he focuses on her pleasure and does not disclose his female genitals. But Lana sees his cleavage down his shirt, and begins to suspect something is going on. Yet she shares some details of their encounter with her stoned girlfriends with obvious glee.

They hold a birthday party for Brandon, at which John shows a growing hostility toward him for his newfound intimacy with Lana. Trouble is brewing, and it gets worse when Lana announces she is quitting her job, and wants to go off to Memphis with Brandon and pursue a career as a karaoke singer. But then Brandon gets caught passing one of Candace's checks and gets thrown in jail, where the police uncover his real identity. By this time Lana has accepted him completely, telling him "I don't care if you are half monkey, or half ape, I'm getting you out of here." Meanwhile, Candace has uncovered evidence that he is female. When his name is printed in the paper as Teena Brandon, his secret is out.

Other than Lana, his new little family is appalled, and confronts him about it. He admits he is going through a sexual identity crisis, and Lana's mother asks him to leave. John exposes Brandon's female genitals, then takes Brandon out to a secluded spot, where John and Tom brutally beat and rape him. He reports the attack, but the local sheriff seems more concerned about his trans nature than with their crime, and fails to bring them in.

Brandon shows trust in Lana, by coming clean with her about his made-up past. She asks him "What were you like before all this? Were you like me? Like a girl girl?" Once again acknowledging his trans nature, Brandon responds "Yeah. Like a long time ago. Then I guess I just was like a boy girl."

John and Tom learn that Brandon has reported their assault, and they hunt him down, shooting and stabbing him mercilessly. Lana curls herself around his lifeless body, and stays there for the rest of the night. The film ends with her reading a letter from Brandon, telling her that he is going back to Lincoln but will meet her soon on the road to Memphis, and that he will love her always and forever.

I chose to discuss *Boys Don't Cry* to conclude this book because it is the story of someone trying to find himself, and break free from what others expect him to be, just the kind of story that Cavell would love. Hilary Swank understood her character that way in her remarks on the DVD featurette: "I wasn't trying to define what Teena Brandon was . . . I was trying to play a person who was pursuing a dream." She later characterized it as "a story about finding your true self, and having the courage and the drive to follow through in being that, and living it to its fullest." Her final comment aptly sums it up: "It's a story of love and acceptance, and of being who you really are with all of your heart and every cell in your body . . . and not conforming to what other people think you should be."

Both critics and audiences agree that this is a film that is both disturbing and exhilarating. The first half of it is a rush of adrenaline, driven by Brandon's electrifying personality. As Tom observes before he turns against Brandon: "People like you don't need to do drugs. You hallucinate 24 hours a day." Brandon loves his life as a boy, reveling in his newfound freedom from the constricting expectations a girl must live up to. His enthusiasm leaves no doubt that he has found his proper gender.

Boys Don't Cry is also a tender love story. Lana likes Brandon immediately; he is head and shoulders above all of the lowlifes she hangs around with. "There's just something about him," as she puts it. He is sensitive, and knows how to treat a lady. He cares about her pleasure in their lovemaking more than his own. When it becomes clear that he is transgender, she doesn't care, and accepts him for who he is. She is still willing to go off with him even after the reveal.

Brandon, for his part, is more guarded. He is obviously in the habit of lying, and tells convincing tales of his dad in Memphis, his mom in Hollywood, and his sister, the model. He sweet-talks Lana, expressing his love in praise. But, at first anyway, he doesn't reveal much of himself. When he initially addresses his "difference," he describes himself as a hermaphrodite, having both male and female genitals (for whatever reason).

But once she tells him it doesn't matter what he is, he opens up. He admits that his father is dead, his mother lives in Lincoln, and that he doesn't have a sister who is a model. His acknowledgment of her as the one he loves is completed by these self-revelations. Their effect on each other also calls them to be all they can be. Their dreams are modest: she wants to be a professional karaoke singer, and he wants to be a firefighter. But they agree that they would settle for running a trailer park together.

Based on a true story, *Boys Don't Cry* is an obvious vehicle for condemning the deep-seated prejudices that lead to Brandon's murder. Cavell made some relevant comments when addressing the work of French philosopher Emmanuel Levinas. For Levinas "the relation to the other can be said to begin with my knowledge of myself as a threat to the other, one could say, my knowledge of our vulnerability to each other, abashed by the demand to acknowledge the other" (2005a: 4). But John and Tom give vent to their unabashed hatred and jealousy of Brandon, denying him the most basic form of acknowledgment as a fellow human being: "If I sought a solution to the skeptical problem of acknowledgment of the other in the form, say, of the question 'How can I trust the basis upon which I grant the existence of the other?' I feel I could not do better than to respond 'You shall not kill'" (2005a: 151). His murderers completely deny his humanity by taking his life.

Boys Don't Cry is a truly great Hollywood film, which, like so many other quality Hollywood productions according to Cavell, has the quest of becoming who you are at its emotional center. Brandon's metamorphosis is shown to be the right thing for him, despite the fact that it costs him his life. His search for self-realization is clearly a success, though it is achieved in a social milieu where he dies for it. For any young person at odds with their assigned gender, Brandon's story is both an inspirational and a cautionary tale. Unfortunately, almost twenty years later, we still live in a society where coming out as a transsexual can exact a terrible personal price. Yet like all good tragedies, the film affirms Brandon's resolute attempt at attaining authenticity despite the cost.

Also, it is a romantic tragedy, which shows Brandon finding someone to love him on his own terms. Lana and Brandon acknowledge each other as lovers in both of Cavell's senses of the term: they cherish each other as they are, and reveal themselves to each other with an intimacy they share with no one else. The overall impression the film leaves one with is strangely optimistic . . . Brandon puts himself in a precarious situation that gets him killed (just as his cousin feared). But his tragedy results from the particular set of hostile circumstances, and we read it as such. In other circumstances, coming out as a transgender person need not have cost him his life. This is a key feature of good tragedy as well. If being who you are would lead to your demise no matter the situation, your death is not tragic but merely self-destructive.

I conclude with this analysis of Cavell's concept of acknowledgment because it is such a good example of his Humanism. When I read the passage about seeing another person in pain demanding that we acknowledge it, something clicked. I had one of those "Ah, just so!" moments. I related it to Kant's imperative to respect other persons as ends in themselves. Cavell got at what that respect requires in a uniquely inspirational fashion. Like so much of his work, it made me want to be myself, by showing empathy for my fellow beings. I guess that's why I think of him as a truly therapeutic philosopher.

NOTES

1. This book contained the original versions of "Kierkegaard on Authority and Revelation," and "The Avoidance of Love (External World Skepticism)."
2. For script of *Boys Don't Cry*, see https://www.scripts.com/script/boys_don%27t_cry_4584 (accessed September 29, 2018).

References

Alderman, Harold (1977), *Nietzsche's Gift*, Ohio University Press.
Cavell, Stanley (1971), *The World Viewed: Reflections on the Ontology of Film*, Viking Press.
Cavell, Stanley (1979a), *The World Viewed: Enlarged Edition*, Harvard University Press.
Cavell, Stanley (1979b), *The Claim of Reason: Wittgenstein, Skepticism, Morality and Tragedy*, Clarendon Press.
Cavell, Stanley (1981), *Pursuits of Happiness: The Hollywood Comedy of Remarriage*, Harvard University Press.
Cavell, Stanley (1987), *Disowning Knowledge in Six Plays of Shakespeare*, Cambridge University Press.
Cavell, Stanley (1988), *Themes Out of School: Effects and Causes*, University of Chicago Press.
Cavell, Stanley (1989), *The New Yet Unapproachable America*, Living Batch Press.
Cavell, Stanley (1992), *The Senses of Walden: An Expanded Edition*, University of Chicago Press.
Cavell, Stanley (1996a), Selections from *Conditions Handsome and Unhandsome: The Constitution of Emersonian Perfectionism*, in Stephen Mulhall (ed.) *The Cavell Reader*, Blackwell.
Cavell, Stanley (1996b), *Contesting Tears: The Hollywood Melodrama of the Unknown Woman*, University of Chicago Press.
Cavell, Stanley (1996c), "Being Odd, Getting Even," in Stephen Mulhall (ed.) *The Cavell Reader*, Blackwell.
Cavell, Stanley (1996d [1969]), "Kierkegaard on Authority and Revelation," in Stephen Mulhall (ed.) *The Cavell Reader*, Blackwell.
Cavell, Stanley (1996e [1969]), "The Avoidance of Love (External World Skepticism)," in Stephen Mulhall (ed.) *The Cavell Reader*, Blackwell.
Cavell, Stanley (1996f [1972]), *The Senses of Walden*, reprinted Stephen Mulhall (ed.) *The Cavell Reader*, Blackwell.
Cavell, Stanley (1996g [1986]), "Being Odd, Getting Even," reprinted in Stephen Mulhall (ed.) *The Cavell Reader*, Blackwell.
Cavell, Stanley (1996h [1987]), "Psychoanalysis and Cinema," reprinted in Stephen Mulhall (ed.) *The Cavell Reader*, Blackwell.
Cavell, Stanley (1996i [1990]), "Epilogue: Everyday Aesthetics," in Stephen Mulhall (ed.) *The Cavell Reader*, Blackwell.
Cavell, Stanley (1996j), "Knowing and Acknowledging," in Stephen Mulhall (ed.) *The Cavell Reader*, Blackwell.

Cavell, Stanley (1999), interviewed in *Harvard Review of Philosophy*, accessed July 26, 2018 at http://www.hcs.harvard.edu/~hrp/issues/1999/Cavell.pdf.

Cavell, Stanley (2004), *Cities of Words: Pedagogical Letters on a Register of the Moral Life*, Harvard University Press.

Cavell, Stanley (2005a), *Philosophy the Day After Tomorrow*, Harvard University Press.

Cavell, Stanley (2005b), "The Good of Film," in William Rothman (ed.) *Cavell on Film*, SUNY Press.

Cavell, Stanley (2005c [1979]) "What Becomes of Things on Film?" in William Rothman (ed.) *Cavell on Film*, SUNY Press.

Cavell, Stanley (2005d [1981]), "North by Northwest," reprinted in William Rothman (ed.) *Cavell on Film*, SUNY Press.

Cavell, Stanley (2005e [1983]), "The Thought of Movies," in William Rothman (ed.) *Cavell on Film*, SUNY Press.

Cavell, Stanley (2005f [1985]), "What Photography Calls Thinking," in William Rothman (ed.) *Cavell on Film*, SUNY Press.

Cavell, Stanley (2005g [1986]), "The Fantastic of Philosophy," in William Rothman (ed.) *Cavell on Film*, SUNY Press.

Cavell, Stanley (2005h [1988]), "Two Cheers for Romance," reprinted in William Rothman (ed.) *Cavell on Film*, SUNY Press.

Cavell, Stanley (2005i [1996]), "Something Out of the Ordinary," in *Cavell on Film*, edited by William Rothman, SUNY Press.

Cavell, Stanley (2005j [1998]), "The World as Things," in William Rothman (ed.) *Cavell on Film*, SUNY Press.

Cavell, Stanley (2005k [2001]), "Moral Reasoning," reprinted in William Rothman (ed.) *Cavell on Film*, SUNY Press.

Emerson, Ralph Waldo (n.d.) *Self-Reliance and Other Essays*, Dover Kindle.

Mill, John Stuart (1862), "The Contest in America," *Fraser's Magazine*, February, accessed February 19, 2019 at https://quod.lib.umich.edu/m/moa/abj5575.0001.001/5?page=root;rgn=full+text;size=100;view=image.

Nietzsche, Friedrich (1878), *Human, All Too Human*, translated by Alexander Harvey, Amazon Kindle Edition, 2011.

Nietzsche, Friedrich (1888), "Beyond Good and Evil," in *The Basic Writings of Nietzsche* (1992), trans. Walter Kaufmann. Modern Library.

Shaw, Daniel (2017), "Stanley Cavell on the Magic of the Movies," *Film-Philosophy*, Vol. 21, Issue 1, 114–32.

Thoreau, Henry David, "On the Duty of Civil Disobedience," in *The Complete Works of Henry David Thoreau* (Kindle Edition) Locations 39, 122–39, 131.

Index

Academy Awards, 17–18, 23, 64, 146
acknowledgment, 3, 5, 9, 54, 61, 66, 80, 95–8, 99, 151–9
action films, 22–3
Adam's Rib (1949), 68, 141
adrenaline, 22–3, 24
aesthetic distance, 8, 22
affirmation, 33, 46–7, 48–9, 50, 95, 110
Ahn, Philip, 127
Alderman, Harold, 55
All Quiet on the Western Front (1930), 124
All the President's Men (1976), 40
Allen, Woody, 4, 105–6, 111
Allwyn, Astrid, 145
American Beauty (1999), 17
American Civil War, 123, 134
American Dream, 2
Andreas-Salome, Lou, 56
Another Woman (1988), 4, 105–6, 111–17
anti-war films, 18–24, 124
"Archaic Torso of Apollo, The" (Rilke), 112
Ariadna, Nina, 101
Aristotle, 24, 66, 110, 142
Arnold, Edward, 144
art, 10, 12, 44–5, 106–10, 111, 112, 114
Arthur, Jean, 145, 147
ascetic ideal, 45, 46
Astaire, Fred, 12, 26–7
atheism, 50
atomic bomb, 123
Austin, J. L., 12, 34–5, 96
auteur theory, 7–8
authenticity, 4, 16, 27, 30, 34, 107–9, 111–12, 116–17, 131
"Avoidance of Love (External World Skepticism)" (Cavell), 141, 152–3
Awful Truth, The (1937), 12, 32, 60, 62

Bavasso, Julie, 98
Bazín, Andre, 8–9, 19, 23–4
Being and Nothingness (Sartre), 96
Being and Time (Heidegger), 106, 109–10
being-for-others, 96
"Being Odd, Getting Even" (Cavell), 42
Bello, Maria, 101
Bentham, Jeremy, 119, 121
Bergman, Ingrid, 79
Beyond Good and Evil (Nietzsche), 48, 54–5, 73
Bigelow, Kathryn, 18–24
Boal, Mark, 22
Boone, Richard, 125
Bordwell, David, 10
Bosco, Philip, 113
Boyer, Charles, 79
Boys Don't Cry (1999), 5, 18, 151, 154–9
bragging, 130–3, 139
Brand, Neville, 126
Brister, Julie, 101
Buchman, Sidney, 146
"Building, Dwelling, Thinking" (Heidegger), 107

Campion, Jane, 52
canon formation, 7–8, 9–10
Capra, Frank, 5, 11, 141, 144–50
Captive, La (2000), 18
Carey, Harry, 147
Carrey, Jim, 71
Carroll, Noël, 9–10
categorical imperative, 30, 120
certainty, 94–6, 98, 152
Cider House Rules, The (1999), 18
Cities of Words (Cavell), 5, 14–18, 27–8, 31–5, 43–6, 48–50, 60, 66, 68, 83, 96–7, 109, 119–21, 131–3, 140–4

civil disobedience, 5, 129, 133–9
Claim of Reason, The (Cavell), 47, 94, 95, 119, 130–1, 141
Clift, Montgomery, 87
cogito, 79
Coleridge, Samuel Taylor, 119, 121
community, 31
Conditions Handsome and Unhandsome (Cavell), 28–9
conformity, 5, 17, 24, 27, 29–30, 43, 47–51, 57, 84–5, 108–9, 122
consent of the governed, 5, 133–5, 140–4, 150
consistency, 30, 72
Contesting Tears (Cavell), 4, 9, 10, 12, 29–31, 46–8, 58–9, 70–1, 76–86, 91, 96, 116, 120, 153, 154
conversation, 3, 29, 57, 60–2, 65, 69, 71, 72, 84, 97, 107, 110
corruption, 5, 98, 144–50
Crouse, Lindsay, 99
culture, 12–13, 43, 44–5, 49, 51

dance, 12, 26–7
Danner, Blythe, 115
Davis, Bette, 80, 110
DeHavilland, Olivia, 86
democracy, 5, 119–20, 135, 136–9, 141–50
Dennis, Sandy, 111
deontological theories, 28, 120
Descartes, René, 79, 95, 141, 152
desire, 15, 29, 59, 60, 69, 121, 122
despair, 10–11, 16, 24, 33, 110, 132–3, 134
didacticism, 15
Disowning Knowledge in Six Plays of Shakespeare (Cavell), 96
divorce, 20, 59, 61, 62, 69, 107, 116
Doll's House, A (Ibsen), 56
Douglas, Kirk, 13
Dunne, Irene, 12
Dunst, Kirsten, 72
duty, 4, 15, 28, 29, 30, 120
DuVernay, Ava, 129, 139

Ecce Homo (Nietzsche), 42
edification, 33, 107
education, 30, 31, 51, 58, 60, 62–3, 68, 70–1, 132
Eisenstein, Sergei, 8
Ejobo, Carmen, 138
elitism, 13, 17, 49–50
Emerson, Ralph Waldo, 11, 13, 14, 24–35, 40–4, 46–52, 57, 66, 77, 80–1, 85, 106, 108–10, 120–2, 132; *see also* perfectionism
empiricism, 29, 132

eternal recurrence, 46–7, 48, 70, 75
Eternal Sunshine of the Spotless Mind (2004), 3, 71–5
everyday life, 10, 18, 24, 26, 35, 97, 107–9
existence *see* human existence
"Experience" (Emerson), 31, 47, 51
expressionism, 8, 9

"Fantastic of Philosophy, The" (Cavell), 97, 108
fantasy, 9, 24
Farrow, Mia, 111
feminism, 16–17, 40, 52, 68, 70–1, 82, 84, 106
Fontaine, Joan, 79
forgetting, 68, 71–5, 97
forgiveness, 60, 61, 62–3, 68, 75, 97
freedom of speech, 121, 147
friendship, 31–2, 46, 56, 60, 62, 65, 66–7, 78

Gardiner, Reginald, 126
Gaslight (1944), 18, 79, 84, 92, 98, 119, 154
Gay Science, The (Nietzsche), 43, 47
gender equality, 61, 68, 71, 153
Genealogy of Morals, The (Nietzsche), 47, 48
genius, 17, 26, 31, 34, 43, 51
Geraghty, Brian, 19
Goliath (2016), 4, 94, 98, 101–3
"Good of Film, The" (Cavell), 17–18, 40
"Good of Movies, The" (Cavell), 14–15
Good Will Hunting (1997), 17
goodness, 2, 15–18, 40, 49
Goranson, Alicia, 155
Grant, Cary, 12, 62, 69
Greenwood, Bruce, 35

Hackman, Gene, 113
Halls of Montezuma (1951), 5, 119, 124–8
Hamlet (Shakespeare), 24, 96
Hanks, Tom, 36, 124
happiness, 5, 10–11, 24–5, 28, 45, 55, 57, 59, 60, 68–71, 83, 120–2, 128, 143–4
Harvard Review of Philosophy interview, 34
hedonic calculus, 5, 15, 121, 123, 126, 128
Hegel, G. W. F., 61, 153
Heidegger, Martin, 4, 8, 16, 27–8, 30–1, 43, 48, 50, 96, 105–12, 116, 132, 153
Heiress, The (1949), 4, 79, 86–92, 154
Henreid, Paul, 81
Hepburn, Katharine, 62, 141
hermeneutic circle, 10
high culture, 12, 44–5
higher self, 3, 52, 54–5
Hitchcock, Alfred, 11
Hobbes, Thomas, 98, 142
Holm, Ian, 111

Homeier, Skip, 125
Hopkins, Miriam, 86
Howard, John, 62
Human, All Too Human (Nietzsche), 51, 57
human existence, 44, 47, 50, 52, 66, 78–9, 96–7, 131, 153, 158
Hume, David, 85
Hunter, Holly, 52
Hurt, William, 101
Hurt Locker, The (2009), 2, 18–24
Hylton, Richard, 125

Ibsen, Henrik, 56
individualism, 2, 5, 31, 45, 52, 122
infantile level of response, 12, 16–17
infidelity, 63–4, 96, 115
Iraq War, 19–24
It Happened One Night (1934), 61

Jackson, Jimmie Lee, 137
Jefferson, Thomas, 143, 144
Johnson, Lyndon, 136–8
Jordan, Louis, 79
justice system, 4, 98–104

Kant, Immanuel, 4, 8, 15, 28, 29, 30, 120, 123, 159
Kaufmann, Walter, 43
Keitel, Harvey, 52
Kennedy, John F., 36, 37
Kibbee, Guy, 144
Kierkegaard, Søren, 16, 46, 119
"Kierkegaard on Authority and Revelation" (Cavell), 119
King, Martin Luther, 5, 129, 134–9
King Lear (Shakespeare), 3, 96, 141, 152–3
"Knowing and Acknowledging" (Cavell), 153
Korean War, 124, 128
Kuhn, Thomas, 93
Kumagai, Frank, 126

Lacan, Jacques, 16
Lady Eve, The (1941), 60, 68
language, 31, 49–50, 97, 107–9, 131
laughter, 46
legal profession, 4, 93–4, 98–104
"Letter from a Birmingham Jail" (King), 136
Letter from an Unknown Woman (1948), 79–80, 84, 92, 154
Letts, Tracy, 36
Levinas, Emmanuel, 158
Lincoln, Abraham, 135, 145, 147
Little Man Tate (1991), 17

Locke, John, 5, 133, 140–4, 150
Lumet, Sidney, 94, 98

Mackie, Anthony, 20
magic, 8, 10–11, 17, 93
Malden, Karl, 125
male gaze, 16–17
Mann, Thomas, 11
marriage, 3–4, 9, 11, 17, 46–7, 52–75, 77–8, 95, 97, 107, 110–11, 113, 115–16, 141–2, 153; *see also* remarriage comedies; romance
Mason, James, 99
melodramas of unknown women, 3–4, 15, 17, 26, 32, 47–8, 52, 57, 76–92, 97–8, 110–11, 116, 154
memory, 71–5, 115–16
metaphysics, 44, 50
Mexican War, 133–4
Milestone, Lewis, 124
Mill, John Stuart, 4–5, 15, 28, 30, 118–23
Milton, John, 71, 142
Mr. Smith Goes to Washington (1939), 5, 141, 144–50
Mitchell, Thomas, 146
montage, 8–9
"Moral Reasoning" (Cavell), 108
moral theory, 28–9, 49, 120–1
Must We Mean What We Say? (Cavell), 95, 152
myths, 10–12, 93, 98, 110, 131–2, 139

narcissism, 96
Neill, Sam, 52
New Deal, 143
"New England Reformers" (Emerson), 33
New Yet Unapproachable America, The (Cavell), 31, 32, 106, 108
New York Times, 35–8
Newman, Paul, 98
Nietzsche, Friedrich, 3, 26, 28, 29, 33, 42–57, 70, 73, 75, 83–4, 107, 108–10, 120
Nietzsche's Gift (Alderman), 55
nihilism, 33, 47, 48–9, 55, 107, 110
Nixon, Richard, 36–40
North by Northwest (1959), 71
"North by Northwest" (Cavell), 71
Now, Voyager (1942), 15, 30, 32, 48, 52, 56, 80–4, 86, 92, 98, 110–11, 154

Olympia (1938), 13
On Liberty (Mill), 5, 120, 122
"On the Duty of Civil Disobedience" (Thoreau), 5, 129, 133–5

ordinary language philosophy, 12, 34–5
"Origin of the Work of Art, The" (Heidegger), 106, 109
originality, 43–4, 49, 50
Oscars *see* Academy Awards
Othello (Shakespeare), 96
Overman *see* Übermensch
Oversoul, 33, 43
Oyelowo, David, 136

Palance, Jack, 125
Pale Criminal, 45
"Panther, The" (Rilke), 112
Paquin, Anna, 52
Paths of Glory (1957), 13
patriotism, 118, 123, 134, 144
Paulson, Sarah, 38
Pearce, Guy, 19
Pentagon Papers, 35–40
perfectionism, 2–4, 15–18, 23, 25–35, 40–1, 47–8, 50, 52, 54, 58–9, 66, 85, 108–9, 120–2, 130, 142, 153
perspectivism, 29, 83–4
Phaedrus (Plato), 107
Philadelphia Story, The (1940), 62–70
philistinism, 49
Philosophical Investigations (Wittgenstein), 94, 96–7
Philosophy the Day After Tomorrow (Cavell), 12–13, 51, 60, 94–5, 98, 153–4, 158
photographic images, 8–9
Piano, The (1993), 3, 52–7
Pindar, 43
Plato, 2, 30, 44, 97, 107
play, 60, 69
Plimpton, Martha, 112
Pope, Alexander, 74
popular culture, 12, 44–5
Pork Chop Hill (1959), 124
Post, The (2017), 3, 35–40
postmodernism, 45, 75
"Preacher, The" (Emerson), 33
privacy, 5, 121
pro-war films, 4–5, 124–8
"Psychoanalysis and Cinema" (Cavell), 46, 61–3
Pursuits of Happiness (Cavell), 3, 33–5, 45, 46, 48–9, 51, 57, 59–61, 77, 86, 119, 140–1

racial equality, 136–9
Rains, Claude, 80, 145
Rampling, Charlotte, 99
Rawls, John, 49, 143
Raymonde, Tania, 101

ready-to-hand viewpoints, 8
realism, 2, 8–9, 18–19, 22–4
"redemptive lawyer" films, 4, 93–4, 98–104
Reeb, James, 138
religion, 34, 45, 47–8, 50, 130, 137
remarriage comedies, 3–4, 11, 15, 17, 26, 28, 32, 35, 45–8, 52, 56–75, 77–8, 97, 107, 110–11, 120, 140–2, 153–4; *see also* marriage; romance
Renner, Jeremy, 19
repetition, 46–7, 61, 70, 75
"Repetition" (Kierkegaard), 46
repression, 52, 66, 77–82, 86–91, 97–8, 110, 154
Republic (Plato), 30
revenge, 46, 59–60, 68, 70, 75, 79–80, 84, 86, 92, 96, 102
revolution, 134, 143–4
Rhys, Matthew, 35
Richardson, Ralph, 86
Riefenstahl, Leni, 13
Rilke, Rainer Maria, 109, 112
Rogers, Ginger, 27
romance, 3, 9, 11, 47, 52, 59–60, 68–9, 71–5, 81–3, 87–92, 97, 107, 110, 141, 153; *see also* marriage; remarriage comedies
romantic comedies *see* remarriage comedies
Romanticism, 43, 48, 52, 97, 106, 119, 121, 131
Roth, Tim, 136
Rowlands, Gena, 111
Ruffalo, Mark, 72

sacred affirmative, 33, 110
sacrifice, 4–5, 23, 78, 82, 84, 119, 123–8
Sarsgaard, Peter, 155
Sartre, Jean-Paul, 96
Saving Private Ryan (1998), 22, 123–4
Schlegel, Friedrich, 106
"Schopenhauer as Educator" (Nietzsche), 43–4, 49
Searching for Bobby Fischer (1993), 17
Second Treatise of Government (Locke), 143–4
self-denial, 45, 110
self-realization, 2–4, 11, 15–18, 25–32, 43–4, 48, 51–7, 62–3, 69, 77–86, 97, 108–9, 111, 119, 154–9
self-reliance, 2, 27, 29–30, 34, 50, 51, 54, 108
Self-Reliance (Emerson), 30, 34, 50
Selma (2014), 5, 129, 136–9
Senses of Walden, The (Cavell), 26, 33, 34, 110, 119, 121–2, 129–32, 152
Sevigny, Chloe, 155
sexism, 38, 40, 68, 70–1

Sexton, Brendan, 155
Shakespeare, William, 10, 24, 95–6, 107, 141, 152–3
Shaw, George Bernard, 49
Sixth Sense, The (1999), 17
skepticism, 4–5, 9–11, 17, 47–8, 61, 77–9, 93–104, 107, 110–11, 123, 132, 139, 141, 152, 154
slavery, 123, 133–5
Socrates, 28, 107
solipsism, 152
"Something Out of the Ordinary" (Cavell), 95
specificity thesis, 9–10, 23–4
Spielberg, Steven, 3, 35
spirituality, 33–4, 130
state of nature, 98, 142, 143
Stella Dallas (1937), 84–5, 92, 98, 154
Stewart, Jimmy, 62, 64, 144
Streep, Meryl, 35
Sturges, Preston, 68
"Subjection of Women, The" (Mill), 119
suspension of disbelief, 2, 9, 17, 24, 97
Swank, Hilary, 154, 157
sympathy, 153
Symposium (Plato), 107

teleological theories, 28, 49, 120–1
Themes Out of School (Cavell), 7, 14–15, 17, 25, 68–71
they-self, 16, 48, 107–9, 111, 114
Thirlby, Olivia, 102
Thoreau, Henry David, 5, 13, 16, 24, 28, 32–5, 43, 54, 69, 77, 123, 129–35, 138–9
Thornton, Billy Bob, 98
"Thought of Movies, The" (Cavell), 12, 13–14, 26–7, 71
"Three Metamorphoses" (Nietzsche), 29, 33, 48–9, 70, 110
Thus Spoke Zarathustra (Nietzsche), 33, 46, 47, 48–9, 55, 70, 110
Tractatus Logico-Philosophicus (Wittgenstein), 96
Tracy, Spencer, 141
tragedy, 10, 95–6, 152–3, 158–9
transcendentalism, 15, 33–4, 50
transfiguration, 15, 43, 71, 76, 77, 80–2, 85–6, 91–2, 110
transgender individuals, 5, 151, 154–9
Truman, Harry, 123
Trump, Donald, 5, 40
truth, 50, 106, 119, 121, 153

Twilight of the Idols (Nietzsche), 43
typicality, 11–12
tyranny, 119

Übermensch, 3, 43, 50, 51, 55–6, 70
"Untimely Meditations" (Nietzsche), 43–4
utilitarianism, 4–5, 29, 30, 119–28, 143
Utilitarianism (Mill), 122
utility, principle of, 30, 120

Verdict, The (1982), 4, 94, 98–101
Vietnam War, 23, 35–40, 124
voice, 16–17, 26, 36, 39, 43–4, 47, 52–6, 77–80, 83–91, 97–8, 109, 116, 131, 141–2, 154
voter registration, 136–9
Voting Rights Act, 5, 138–9

Wagner, Robert, 125
Walden (Thoreau), 5, 129, 130–3
Walk in the Sun, A (1945), 124
Wallace, George, 136–7
war, 2, 4–5, 18–24, 118–19, 123
Warden, Jack, 99
Washington Post, 35–40, 137
Watergate, 40
Webb, Jack, 125
"What Becomes of Things on Film?" (Cavell), 97, 121
What is Called Thinking (Heidegger), 106, 108, 110
"What Photography Calls Thinking" (Cavell), 48
whimsy, 26
Widmark, Richard, 124
Wilkinson, Tom, 73, 136
Will to Power, 51, 54–5
Wilson, Janis, 82
Winfrey, Oprah, 136
Winslet, Kate, 71
Winter, Sarah, 101
Wittgenstein, Ludwig, 4, 12, 16, 28, 34–5, 84, 93–8, 106, 107
Wood, Elijah, 72
"World as Things, The" (Cavell), 50–1, 107–8, 109–10
World Viewed, The (Cavell), 2, 7–13, 18, 80
World War II, 123–8, 150

Yokum, Dwight, 102
Yulin, Harris, 112

EU representative:
Easy Access System Europe
Mustamäe tee 50, 10621 Tallinn, Estonia
Gpsr.requests@easproject.com

www.ingramcontent.com/pod-product-compliance
Lightning Source LLC
Chambersburg PA
CBHW071848230426
43671CB00012B/2101